The North Pennines:
Landscape and Legend

Iain Brown

Published by Summary House Publications
Summary House, Woodland, DL13 5RH

Printed by Lintons Printers, Crook, Co. Durham DL15 8RA

Text and Photographs are Copyright © Iain Brown 2006

All rights reserved. No part of this publication may be reproduced in a retrieval system, or transmitted, in any form or by any means, electronic or mechanical, by photocopying, recording or otherwise, without prior permission in writing from the publisher.

ISBN   0-9553588-0-9
         978-0-9553588-0-7

A CIP catalogue record for this book is available from the British Library.

Front cover: Tunstall Reservoir
Title page: Fog with 'Brocken Spectre', Devil's Water
Frontispiece: Hay meadows, Widdybank
Contents: Steam engine, South Tynedale Railway
Back Cover: Brough Castle

SUNDERLAND CITY LIBRARIES	
K2748413 008	
Bertrams	02.03.07
942.8BRO	£18.95
WTC	PO-613

Acknowledgements

The following authors and publishers are thanked for permission to use copyright material: Bill Mitchell for the extract from 'The Changing Dales'; Charlie Emett and Sutton Publishing for lines from 'Discovering the Eden Valley'; the Wainwright Estate and Frances Lincoln Publishers for extracts from 'A Pennine Journey'; Faber and Faber for quotes from the work of WH Auden.

Many people have provided help and advice during the preparation of this book. Special thanks are due to Jean Brown, George Brown, Lesley Snowball, Ken Snowball, Claire Nicolson and Leila, Gary Brown, Anne Brown, Sheila Jones, Stan Jones, Nenthead Mine Centre, Shane Harris (North Pennines AONB), and the staff of Barnard Castle public library. Ian Fothergill of Lintons Printers has been an enthusiastic supporter during the production process.

Contents

Introduction 1

Making of the Landscape I: Natural History 7

Making of the Landscape II: Human History 14

Stainmore and Upper Eden 21

Eden and East Fellside 31

Lower Teesdale and Greta 49

Upper Teesdale 65

Weardale 81

Derwentdale and Devil's Water 99

The Allendales 113

South Tynedale 129

Geltsdale 145

Bibliography 148

Index 150

Introduction

Oh, my heart is fain to hear the soft wind blowing,
Soughing through the tree tops up on northern fells.
Oh, my eyes an ache to see the brown burns flowing,
Through the peaty soil and tinkling heather bells.

Ada Smith (1876 - 1898)

This pictorial blend of description, interpretation and folklore has as its inspiration a tranquil but expansive area of upland forming the northern section of the Pennine hills. It aims to explore the wider landscape of this district, introducing some of its rich diversity and venturing beyond those few sites that have become 'honeypot' tourist attractions. The itinerary is based upon the main dales but deviates to include towns and villages, castles and abbeys, streams and fells, lakes and forests. Throughout the tour, and beginning with the introductory chapters, the opportunity is taken to consider the different factors that have shaped the scenery we see today: from its distinctive natural history to the human landscape consequent upon many millennia of people living and working in the uplands.

> **'The Pennines'**
>
> The Pennines are, of course, the long chain of hills running through Northern England from the Peak District to the Tyne-Solway Gap. The actual name, however, appears to be an 18th century invention, devised by Charles Bertram during scholarly activities researching Roman Britain. The lack of source material led Bertram to produce a highly-detailed but fictional manuscript that described the long mountain range in the north as the *'Alpes Penina'*. Although the comparison had been made before, notably by William Camden in the 16th century (and the writer Daniel Defoe had compared them to The Andes), the medieval manuscript provided a seemingly solid foundation for the name. When the anglicised form was adopted by the early geologists, it soon entered into common usage.

How do we define the area of the North Pennines? Difficulties can often occur with such definitions because administrative districts typically do not equate with more natural descriptions based on the 'lie of the land'. Topographers have tended to distinguish the southern Pennines (including the Peak District) from the northern Pennines using the broad depression of the 'Aire Gap' near Skipton in Yorkshire. The definition used in this book is more specific and restrictive, recognising the North Pennines as a distinctive upland area to the north of the Yorkshire Dales, thereby following the normal use of both these terms nowadays (although another modern idiosyncrasy is that not all of the 'Yorkshire Dales' are now in Yorkshire!). This characterization also concurs with the befitting designation in 1988 of a large section of these uplands as the North Pennines Area of Outstanding Natural Beauty (AONB), albeit a rather belated official recognition of their high landscape qualities compared to the four national parks previously established in Northern England.

The adopted geographic definition can be amply justified by the peculiar character of these northern uplands compared to neighbouring districts such as the Yorkshire Dales. Both the physical landscape, which is underlain by a single structural unit known as the Alston Block, and its human history, which has been strongly influenced by the resources and constraints of the uplands, are generally quite distinct. In terms of boundaries, the southern and northern limits are therefore prescribed by the pass of Stainmore and the Solway-Tyne Gap respectively, with the western boundary being the Eden valley. However, in the east there is more of a transition zone as the uplands decline into the ridges and plains of the Durham coalfield. Within these boundaries, the intention has been to be inclusive rather than exclusive. The arbitrary limits defined by the official AONB unfortunately exclude much interesting scenery around the edges, therefore the itinerary aims to seek out and include these neglected margins to restore a more natural balance.

Within the core of the defined area, settlements are generally small and much of the land is sparsely populated, with Middleton-in-Teesdale, Stanhope, Alston and Allendale Town being the main foci. Nevertheless, a series of attractive towns are located in the lowland transition zone around the periphery of the hills, each having important links with their surroundings. In the Eden valley are Appleby and Kirkby Stephen, whilst the northern fringes have Brampton, Haltwhistle and Hexham. The eastern slopes eventually end in the more populous coalfield towns but both Wolsingham and Barnard Castle have a long history characterising them as typical Pennine market towns.

In general terms, the upland spine of the North Pennines forms a crudely-shaped 'K' with Cross Fell acting as the hub. The main Pennine watershed between east- and west-flowing rivers is defined by a broad ridge extending north-west from Stainmore over a series of major summits to finally terminate at the Solway-Tyne Gap. The western side of this watershed falls abruptly to the Eden valley in a steep slope *(the Pennine Escarpment)* extending the full length of the range. By contrast, the slopes to the east decline much more gradually with further areas of high ground. As a consequence, the two other branches of the 'K' gradually diverge on this eastern side of the watershed, with the southernmost forming a broad uplift between Teesdale and Weardale. The northernmost branch is more complicated, and actually splits into a series of subsidiary ridges separating the valley of the South Tyne from those containing the West Allen, East Allen, Devil's Water and Derwent rivers.

The broad horizons of the North Pennines, from Cross Fell

The upland core of the North Pennines has sometimes been described as 'England's last great wilderness'. Here are the loftiest summits of the Pennines, including Cross Fell the highest at 893m above sea level, and the largest area of uninhabited and uncultivated wild land. South of the Scottish Border, there is nowhere else with such large expanses of open high ground, much of it being remote from human habitation or roads. This is especially the case on some of the vast sweeping fells and moors on the eastern side of the watershed, notably on Stainmore Common, or the area around Mickle Fell, or the large expanse of high land to the east of Cross Fell forming the headwaters of the Tees. Further north, the desolation of Whitfield Moor or the land north of Hartside Cross also share the same characteristics. One can certainly wander for miles across these uplands without seeing another soul. Horizons are wide, landscapes are broad, and skies are big.

Yet, in general, this is not a 'wilderness' area when considered in the truest sense of the term. Such a description would imply a pristine landscape untouched by human impacts and therefore remaining in its original primeval state. The most obvious objection to such a proclamation is that the ancient forest formerly covering most of the land has gone, which can be attributed mainly to the actions of mankind abetted by the changing postglacial climate. Furthermore, other human-induced changes have also significantly affected the North Pennine landscape, to a greater degree than in most other upland areas. In times past, this was an area of considerable industrial activity that reached high onto the fells. Relics of mining and quarrying are abundant: whilst now being slowly reclaimed by nature, they have often significantly modified the original landscape, including its topography and vegetation.

People have therefore long been an integral and important part of this landscape. Although the fells may be quieter now, hill farms maintain their large flocks of sheep that graze the valley intakes and the rough swards above. Large sections of the uplands are also managed for grouse, with the heather regularly burnt to retain a young vigorous growth and the moors often drained by systems of artificial ditches ('grips'). Most of the original natural landscape has therefore gone, replaced by a semi-natural environment that is now in its most tranquil human phase for many centuries. Those fragments of the ancient landscape that do remain are either hidden in deep wooded ravines or isolated on the thin limestone rocks and soils which have maintained their postglacial flora. Both of these relict landscapes therefore deserve to be doubly-celebrated for their remarkable natural heritage.

An apt metaphor for interpreting the evolution of the landscape over time is to see it as a palimpsest, the parchment used in medieval times for producing manuscripts. The same palimpsest would be used many times over and again

INTRODUCTION

because of the scarcity of the material, but although some scraping and cleaning occurred before each successive overwriting, previous documents could still often be visible beneath the current version. Both the physical and human characteristics of the landscape can be 'read' just like the palimpsest, with multiple layers imprinted sequentially over and over again. The most recent pages may be the most visible now, but impressions also remain from the past, potentially providing a link with distant happenings which have otherwise been lost. The landscape can therefore provide a memory of past events that is intimately linked to its present form and structure, so giving the scenery of today a fascinating extra dimension. Sometimes these features can be seen directly and are therefore virtually indelible, whilst in other places they are much more faint and fading. This multi-layering aspect of the landscape is particularly characteristic of the North Pennines. For those that take the time to 'read' the palimpsest and consider the implications, it provides a subtle yet abiding interest that make this part of the country such a rewarding place to explore.

Lead mining landscape: Pikelaw, Upper Teesdale.

T'Awd Man

Amongst the upland landscapes of the North Pennines, man's former presence is a particularly distinctive feature of the scenery at many localities. Relicts from the past provide clues, often enigmatic and puzzling, to those who once lived and worked there, frequently in very harsh conditions. The miners who eked a living both underground and on the surface also recognised a shadowy presence from the past: months of backbreaking work in pursuit of a profitable vein could be thwarted by discovering previous workings of which there had been no record or knowledge. Sometimes, noises would be heard deep in the mine or a dim glimmer of candlelight noticed. These activities were the work of the Old Man (T'Awd Man), a figure of respect and wisdom.

After a while, his manifestation in the landscape becomes almost ubiquitous. It then begins to seem that T'Awd Man probed and explored all over these uplands in search of resources and assets that could make life easier. As well as the vegetated spoil heaps and dilapidated lichenous ruins of old mine workings, his existence is shown by the shapely 'curricks' and crude stone shelters located high on the fells, for he could have also been a quarryman or shepherd. Over time, his life would undoubtedly have become adapted to the land, its rocks and contours, its rhythms and seasons. And so, despite no written record, his presence remains today, accompanying all who explore these remote uplands, and gradually forming an enduring association with the landscape.

Currick, Murton Fell (an old guide cairn)

Exploring the Landscape

Walking is the most natural way to explore the landscape at leisure, and the North Pennines is an excellent venue for this activity (although many itineraries can be adapted for cycling, horse-riding or even ski-ing!). Under the 2001 Countryside & Rights of Way Act, most of the uplands are now defined as 'Access Land'. However, the North Pennines have traditionally been spared the public access issues that have occurred in upland areas elsewhere. This reflects the good relations that have developed over time and although legal rights were more limited in the past, this was seldom an issue. To continue this positive state of affairs, a little flexibility may be required occasionally. The vast majority of the people I have met in these uplands have been warm and friendly, many being very interesting characters, typically with a fascinating local knowledge.

The higher fells can be difficult terrain, often remote from habitation. The new Ordnance Survey 1:25000 Pathfinder series are particularly useful both for navigation and for exploring the less obvious features of the landscape. Some of the old mine workings, particularly shafts, are potentially lethal and require extra caution. An early misfortune of this type occurred in 1641 to Roger Grummel of Hightharpe, who was lost 'at a shaft on Tan Hill by falling to the bottom and dyed'. As indicated by other tragic accidents that have occurred more recently, the risks remain. In addition, the Warcop Artillery Range has its own rules and regulations, with access restricted to certain days in the year, and this therefore area requires its own arrangements.

Introduction

WH Auden

Always my boy of wish returns
To those peat-stained deserted burns
That feed the Wear and Tyne and Tees
And, turning states to strata, sees
How basalt, long oppressed, broke out
In wild revolt at Cauldron Snout

New Year Letter, 1940

By contrast with the romantic scenery espoused by the Lakes' Poets such as Wordsworth and Southey, the landscapes of the North Pennines were a major inspiration to the 20th century poet WH Auden. In particular, he had a deep interest in the rocks and industrial relics of the lead-mining districts, with one of his favourite books being Westgarth Forster's seminal study of the geology and early mining history. Many of his poems draw upon this inspiration, as manifest in a particular conjugation or rhythmic grouping of words in his own inimitable style. For example, sparse and reflective language captures the poignant and often melancholy state of the old workings. To Auden, part of the fascination of the mines was the introspection which they engendered, with a recurrent theme being their inevitable mortality: the frenetic activity of the boom years leading to predictable decline, and now the slow gradual return to nature.

Another inspiration for Auden was the peculiar limestone landscapes of the Pennines, with their capricious streams and enigmatic landforms. This fascination is particularly celebrated in the famous poem 'In Praise of Limestone', but also represents a familiar theme reappearing throughout many of his other works.

Sikehead Mine, Derwent valley

Old mine workings being gradually reclaimed by nature at Slitt Mine

Making of the Landscape 1: Natural History

Except for children (who don't know enough not to ask the important questions), few of us spend much time wondering why nature is the way it is .... Carl Sagan 1988

The distinctive natural and human history of the North Pennines owes much to its unique geological inheritance, recently recognised by it becoming one of the global *'Geopark'* network that links key interpretative areas worldwide. In particular, the presence of valuable mineral ores and other rocks with a significant economic value has provided a major source of income and employment. The available rocks have also dictated local building styles, varying from the warm red sandstones or brockrams of the Eden valley to the more subdued ochre sandstones and grey limestones in the east. Geology has also been a key influence on soils and farming conditions: limestone soils and glacial valley drifts providing more ecological diversity and a richer pasturage compared to the more common acid soils of the moors.

The basic geological structure of the North Pennines is relatively simple, characterised by the distinctive unit known as the *Alston Block*. This unit is defined by major faults on its western (Eden) and northern (Tyne Gap) edges, separated by the Stainmore depression from a similar unit (the Askrigg Block) to the south, and overlain by the deposits of the Durham coalfield to the east. Most of the rocks were laid down in a thick sedimentary layer-cake sequence during the Carboniferous period. This horizontality is still evident today in the step-and-bench pattern evident on many valley sides due to varying rates of erosion on different rock strata. It is also responsible for the flat tops of most of the hills and for many of the waterfalls. However, when considered on a regional scale the rocks actually form a gentle dome shape due to later folding effects. They have also been disrupted by fault-lines, being particularly clearly buckled along a large north-south fault-line known as the Burtreeford Disturbance. The horizontal simplicity has also been complicated by intrusions of molten magma, forming features known as sills and dykes. Final modifications have been performed by the etching and scouring effect of ice and water, eroding material from some locations and depositing it elsewhere.

A few remnants exist of the earlier rocks pre-dating the Carboniferous, a legacy of the period when the northern and southern parts of Britain joined together into a united landmass. Along the western Pennine escarpment, faulting has exposed a narrow band of lavas, slates and conglomerates known as the *Cross Fell Inlier*. These rocks form the graceful conical peaks of the Pikes and match similar rocks in the Lake District. Another tiny remnant of these rocks exists in Upper Teesdale at Widdybank, where pencils or 'widdys' were fashioned from graphite in the soft slate, again having parallels with the Lakeland pencil industry. At this time magma was present under the mountains, but never reached the surface. Its presence under the North Pennines was confirmed by a borehole at Rookhope in 1961 which discovered granite at a depth of 390m; recent further probings are examining the feasibility of this rock as a source of geothermal energy through hot water.

Horizontal banding of rocks on Bollihope Common

During the Carboniferous, the basin now defined by the Alston Block was gradually subsiding in a warm maritime climate close to the Equator. The earliest deposits were thick almost-pure limestones, presently exposed at a few sites on the Pennine escarpment. After this, a repeated pattern of *cyclothem* sedimentation developed, producing the archetypal Pennine rocks of the *Yoredale Series*. These are represented by the different bands of limestone, sandstone, siltstone and shale that form the stepped profiles on valley sides or the waterfalls in streams, usually due to the limestone rocks being more resistant to erosion.

Cyclothems

Each of the repeated sequences in the Yoredale rocks ('Yoredale' being the old name for Wensleydale where the rocks are particularly well-displayed) is a cyclothem. The cycle would begin with lime-muds in deep water, formed mainly from algae and shelly sea creatures. As these muds accumulated, the sea became shallower and periods of intermittent uplift resulted in eroded material from land being washed out to sea, burying the mud and consolidating it to form limestones. The land margin became closer and coarser sediments began to replace the fine muds, leading to siltstones and sandstones, and eventually the site changed from a marine environment into a coastal river delta. Where river channels crossed the delta, finer silts were deposited and the area became marshy, with vegetation such as ferns and conifers that died to leave peat. With time, consolidation of the lower layers of peat as the pile thickened eventually produced coal; various intermediate layers were also made including fine-grained *fireclays* and *seatearths*, or coarser silica-rich sandstones known as *ganisters*. Most of the surviving coal deposits today are in the thicker later sequences of the Durham coalfield to the east, but small seams exist in the North Pennines, sometimes partly converted by heat into good-quality semi-anthracite, as on Alston Moor, whilst elsewhere lesser quality 'craw-coal' is found. Subsequently the rate of subsidence of the basin would increase again, the sea would return, scouring away much of the peat and coal, and the cycle would return to deep-water limestones. Despite the fragmentary evidence, detailed research has deduced the presence of at least 22 cyclothems in the North Pennines.

Similarly, the typical banded appearance of limestone cliffs is the result of thin layers of mudstone or shale, subsequently eroded out to provide breaks between the limestone beds. Experienced miners and quarrymen could trace these 'posts' from one area to another to help predict the expected sequence at different places, assisted by any fossils present in the rocks.

Ashgill Force: the falls occur over resistant beds of limestone

Fossils occur not only within in-situ limestone outcrops, but also in river cobbles or scree. Amongst those commonly found are animal remains such as crinoids, brachiopods and corals, or various types of plant fossil. Crinoids (often called 'sea lilies') consist of a tough wiry stem formed from nut-and-bolt-like features called *ossicles* (or 'St. Cuthbert Beads'). Brachiopods are scallop-shaped shells found in many varieties, and also present in some sandstones as well as the more normal limestones. Corals are locally abundant where reefs had formed during shallow seas; they occur with particular profusion and density in parts of Weardale, giving the limestone a speckled appearance in the celebrated 'Frosterley Marble'. In addition, traces of animal burrows sometimes occur in sandstones, whilst plant fossils, such as imprints of moss-trees or ferns in seatearths, can also be found in a variety of rocks.

In places, the sandstones were also mixed with platy mica minerals to form thin fissile beds that were often worked in the past to produce flagstone roofing materials, as at Slate Quarry on Stainmore. However, the quarrymen tend to prefer thicker beds of rock with regular transverse joints *(freestone)* so that stone masons can then work it in any direction, producing blocks 2-3m thick. Silica-rich ganister rock has been quarried at various sites, notably at the large excavations of Harthope Quarry (between Teesdale and Weardale), for use as refractory bricks when lining steel furnaces.

During the later stages of the Carboniferous, large deltas built up with thick deposits of coarse sandstone being laid down. This has produced the distinctive *Millstone Grit* series that now covers much of the higher fells, usually by acting as a cap rock on top of the other rocks; as its name suggests, this rock has been the favoured source from which to produce millstones. Also formed at this later stage were thick deposits of shale, sandstone and coal, known collectively as the *Coal Measures*. Although widespread throughout the Durham coalfield, these later deposits have been removed from the uplands of the North Pennines by a period of extensive erosion, but faulting near the Tyne valley has left coalfield outliers at Midgeholme, Plenmeller and Stublick. As well as exploiting these coal seams around the margins of the hills, collieries and other industries have often used the adjacent shales to make bricks or tiles.

Following on from the hot-humid Carboniferous, the Permian period had a very different climate with the conditions remaining hot but becoming very dry. At this time, desert sands accumulated to produce the red Eden sandstones, with large evaporation basins leaving residues of gypsum and anhydrite, now being worked near Kirkby Thore. At the margins of the basins, erosion produced the *brockram* rocks now found around Kirkby Stephen, mixing and cementing lime fragments with sand.

'Frosterley marble': Bollihope Burn

Millstones: Carr Crags

Brockram rocks: Stenkrith

The Whin Sill: High Cup Nick

The basic structure of the Alston Block was then modified both by faulting and by intrusions of molten magma. A particularly significant event squeezed magma in step-like horizontal sheets into the existing rocks to produce the *Great Whin Sill*; the term 'sill' has been adopted by geologists from the old miners' term for hard rocks. The Whin Sill cooled to form the dark, hard, quartz-dolerite rock commonly termed *whinstone*. It outcrops in a broad arc from the crags and waterfalls of Teesdale, where it reaches a maximum thickness of 70m, to the slopes above the Eden valley (e.g. at High Cup and Ardale) then through South Tynedale to the escarpment of the Roman Wall. Quarries have capitalized on economic demand for the high durability of whinstone, notably at Middleton, Dine Holme (Teesdale), Hallbankgate (South Tynedale) and Cowshill (Weardale) on the Great Whin Sill, with a quarry at Stanhope working a thinner branch of the rock *(Little Whin Sill)*.

Many of the rocks adjacent to the Whin Sill were metamorphosed by the heat of the molten magma. Limestone in Teesdale was therefore locally converted into a marble rock commonly referred to as *sugar limestone* because of its coarse granular state. Similarly, sandstones were baked into unusually hard units whilst coal seams were locally converted towards the richer carbon properties of anthracite. Shale was occasionally modified into whetstone, a brittle rock typically used for producing sharpening stones.

As time went on, folding and fracturing of the rocks produced narrow fault-lines along which hot briny solutions could penetrate. This development has been the key factor leading to the unique mineral assemblage of the North Pennines Orefield. One set of faults runs WSW-ENE or SW-NE and tends to have a smooth, clean fracture: these are known the *Lead Veins* because they tend to contain the richest mineral deposits. Another series of faults, running N-S or NW-SE has a larger, more irregular displacement, forming the less ore-rich *Cross Veins*. A less-common third series, termed the *Quarter Set* faults, runs either W-E or NW-SE with small vertical displacements occasionally providing large cavities for minerals to accumulate.

As the briny solutions progressively cooled, different minerals were precipitated out as separate bands within the cavities. As well as ores of lead (galena and cerrusite) or zinc (sphalerite and calamine), other waste or 'gangue' minerals were produced, such as calcite, quartz, fluorite[1] and barytes. Some veins, despite being major features in the landscape, contain very little ore, notably the Great Sulphur Vein on Alston Moor, which has a high proportion of quartz. However, in the limestone beds, some of the surrounding rock was occasionally replaced at the sides

---

[1] Flourite is the mineral form of the rock usually known as fluospar.

of the near-vertical veins to produce broad horizontal ore deposits known as *'flats'*. The Great Limestone, which is typically 20m thick, has become the most economically important rock unit because it tends to contain the richest veins and 'flats'. By contrast, shales and mudstones are barren rocks because the fault-lines along which the mineral fluids penetrated the strata are less well-defined in these softer units.

Two main mineral zones can be recognised: an inner zone centred on upper Weardale in which fluorite is very common and an outer zone where it is replaced by barytes and witherite which form at a lower temperature. This closely matches with the presence of the underlying granite found in the Rookhope borehole suggesting that it supplied the extra heat within the fluorite zone. An interesting property of some of the fluorite is that it is often green-coloured when buried but soon changes to purple when excavated and exposed to sunlight. Following the main phase of mineralisation, a secondary phase then occurred in which groundwater from above mixed with the minerals at lower temperatures causing a process of oxidation. One end-product of this process was iron minerals such as siderite, pyrite and limonite (ochre), which have formed important iron ore deposits in Weardale.

Much more recently, a by-product of volcanic activity in West Scotland has been vertical magma intrusions that cut through the existing rocks as narrow dykes. One of these, the Armathwaite Dyke is prominent in the Eden Valley and extends eastwards across South Tynedale and Teesdale to become the Cleveland Dyke.

Mell Fell and Gasdale from Murton Pike: shakeholes in the limestone show the horizontal beds of the Yoredale series; the dark gash (middle-right) marks the White Mines which worked a near-vertical lead vein cutting the limestone

The final shaping of the land has occurred during the multiple ice ages of the current (Quaternary) geological period. During the last of these glacial episodes, ice overran the district from northwest and west, supplied mainly by the mountains of Scotland and the Lake District. The scouring effect of rocks entrained in the ice carved out deep valleys and basins such as High Cup, with the eroded material then laid down as thick deposits of till (boulder clay) on the valley floors. The regional pattern of ice flow can be reconstructed from the distribution of anomalous boulders known as *erratics*: for example, Robin Hood's Penistone in Lunedale is a sandstone boulder on limestone bedrock. Similarly, the highly-distinctive pink Shap Granite from the eastern fringes of the Lake District has been transported across the Pennines to produce the Boulder Stone in Deepdale (near Barnard Castle), and a house in nearby Cotherstone even has such a boulder built into its walls. By contrast, the massive limestone blocks transported to form the anomalously lush-green knolls of the Bullman Hills, north-west of Cross Fell, suggest that at some stage there was also a small local ice-cap on the highest Pennine tops.

Dry channels created by glacial meltwater above the Eden valley

Ice flow is also revealed by the streamlined hillocks of *drumlins* formed as the glaciers begun to melt but were still able to exert pressure on the ground below. Classic 'basket of egg' drumlin topography exists in the Eden valley, whilst elsewhere these features clearly show where ice was pushed east across Stainmore into Lunedale and Teesdale, and through the Tyne valley near Haltwhistle. Large meltwater channels formed at this stage too, and are typically recognisable as dry channels or deep valleys with a small 'misfit' stream. In some cases, the channels have nicked right through the lowest point of a watershed, such as at Folly Top (near Eggleston), or the channel systems crossing from South Tynedale to Allendale then through to the Derwent valley. Others form sinuous or arcuate etchings on valley sides, such as the numerous features on the East Fellside, with good examples also near Alston and in Teesdale. The melting glaciers also dumped large heaps of irregular material as *moraines* or *kames*, such as the Seven Hills near Bowes. At Gilsland, this deposition diverted the River Irthing westwards to the Eden from its original eastwards course to the Tyne at Greenhead.

Once the glaciers had gone, soils began to develop. Over limestone outcrops, soils became thin but free-draining, contrasting with the acidic waterlogged soils that developed upon the impermeable gritstones and shales. In the valleys, glacial deposits produced a diversity of soil-types depending on the contents of the eroded rocks that they contained. Surface exposure of limestone meant it could be dissolved by rainwater, forming *shakehole* collapse features and caves with underground streams that disappear down *swallow holes*. As the thickness of the limestone beds is less than those found in the Yorkshire Dales, cave systems are less extensive; nevertheless, good examples exist at many places including Moking Hurth (Teesdale), the Fairy Holes and Clints Crags (Weardale), Knock Fell Caverns, and on North Stainmore. In addition, mining operations discovered large caverns at both Hudgill and Ayle (near Alston).

Trees became widespread as the climate ameliorated, with the pioneer species of birch, juniper, willow and pine eventually being succeeded in the more fertile areas by species such as oak and alder after a few millennia. On the thinner limestone soils, hazel continued to be the dominant species. At the postglacial climatic optimum, temperatures were 1.5-2°C higher than at present and conditions were significantly drier.

The present-day climate of the North Pennines reflects its upland location at a significant distance from the sea, and is typically summarised as 'cool and wet'. Areas below 300m usually have a growing season from April to mid-November but temperatures typically drop about 1°C for every 150m of height, therefore the growing season is significantly reduced with altitude. As a result, hay-making in the upper valleys is by necessity rather later in the year than at lower sites. Frosts are common in winter, with an average of 160 air frosts recorded at the weather station on Great Dun Fell. The lowest extreme temperatures, however, occur in sheltered pockets, notably in the Eden valley or at locations such as Allenheads.

The Pennine fells are not quite as wet as the Lake District, but being a significant mountain barrier they nevertheless accumulate considerable annual precipitation totals. Cross Fell receives about 2100mm each year, twice as much as Haltwhistle, Stanhope and Middleton, and is also notable for its persistent hilltop cloud cover. Occasionally, very heavy cloudbursts occur on the hills in the heat of summer producing significant local damage. This is also the snowiest part of England, although winters now are evidently much less harsh than decades ago. In the distant past, horse races have occurred along a frozen river Tees, whilst Mitchell and Richardson skated 30km along the same river in 1880! More recently in 1979, snow was recorded in every month except August. Nevertheless, despite the undoubted effects of global warming, spring blizzards ('lambing snows') still remain a common feature of the Pennine year.

Limestone outcrops, River South Tyne

The biggest change in the postglacial landscape has been the removal of the extensive tree cover which had developed to cover much of the region, except on the highest tops. Its demise was primarily the result of clearance by humans, but the climate had also gradually shifted to its current cool-wet phase, discouraging re-growth. Trunks and roots from the time of widespread forest cover are still visible in peat bogs or stream sections. The recent large-scale development of lead mining in many of the valleys has also significantly modified the behaviour of streams and rivers. Denudation of the vegetation from hillsides and production of large spoil heaps added much additional debris to stream channels leading to the creation of the wide gravelly *'haughs'* that are especially prevalent in Allendale and South Tynedale.

Even today, tundra-like *periglacial* features are maintained on the high fells. Regular freezing of the ground with the growth of ice crystals leads to patterned ground formations as soils are heaved up then released again during the thaw, causing movement and sorting of stones. On the extensive summit plateau of Cross Fell, this is clearly demonstrated by a variety of earth hummocks and stone stripe features, related to the gradient of the slope.

Typical poorly-drained ground, frozen by a sharp frost

Acid soils and poor drainage have produced the characteristic upland vegetation of the North Pennines. Peat has formed where the waterlogged conditions have meant that organic matter has accumulated over time due to the slow rate of decomposition. On the higher wetter areas, mat grass, purple moor grass and cotton grass are prevalent, with bright green sphagnum indicating the wettest bogs; grass often develops into large tussocks (traditionally known as Scotsman's Heads) making walking even more arduous. Better drainage on rocky areas often encourages bilberry or the less common cloudberry (referred to locally as knoutberry). The drier climate of the eastern moors, where the ground can dry out for part of the year, has produced extensive swathes of heather, whilst lower down the hillsides bracken is typically widespread. In places where the Whin Sill outcrops, the mineral soils have encouraged a more unusual flora including juniper and bearberry.

Limestone areas are usually dramatically distinct, with peat absent, and grass swards or rock outcrops containing a much richer flora, including atypical herbaceous plants and some rather rare species. Most notably, a unique combination of factors in Upper Teesdale has encouraged the presence of relict arctic-alpine species producing habitats of international significance. At springs, nutrients leached from the surrounding rocks can become concentrated to produce a vivid 'flush' of lush vegetation. In addition, spoil areas around old lead mines are colonised by specialist plants such as spring sandwort, alpine scurvy-grass and alpine pennycress, with the mountain pansy also often thriving in such adversity.

Riverbanks and meadows can also provide a varied flora and fauna. The restricted spread of the more intensive farming routines into the uplands has meant that many of the old hay meadows have survived, with a remarkably rich diversity compared to the sown pastures produced by modern agriculture. Although much of the original woodland has gone, some relics of the ancient woods have survived in steep-sided stream or river valleys. In these favoured situations, oak, ash, hazel, beech and alder are complemented by birch and rowan in the more marginal areas. Adders and grass snakes are common at preferred sites in some of the valleys, and in summer damselflies and dragonflies patrol the meadows together with butterflies such as the common blue and small copper. By the riverbanks, otters are making a comeback but non-native mink are also spreading through the area. Happily, every stream seems to have a dipper (affectionately know as the 'water piedy') busily flitting in and out of the water, sometimes also accompanied by species such as sandpiper or grey wagtail.

The heather moors are the favoured habitat of grouse and blackcock (black grouse), whilst pheasant and partridge are nurtured in the lower woodlands. Unfortunately, zealous keepering associated with the game birds has resulted in the elimination of many predators that would otherwise occur on the moors. This is particularly evident with regard to the birds of prey, although the hen harrier is now making a slow comeback and merlin are occasionally seen, as well as the more common peregrine, sparrowhawk and kestrel. Short-eared owl and raven are other notable upland species, with a few buzzards in the west. Perhaps the most characteristic birds are the waders, each with their distinctive calls and behaviour. Curlews, lapwings, plovers, snipe, redshank and dunlin are all present, colonising the less-developed farmland as seasonal visitors from spring to autumn. On the high fells occasional dotterel may be seen, whilst on the lower slopes, ring ouzel, meadow pipits, skylarks, wheatears, whinchats and stonechats can be observed. These are just some of the wide range of animal and plant species that can be found in the stream, meadow, wood, moor and bog habitats of the North Pennines (for specialist texts, see *Bibliography*).

Making of the Landscape II: Human History

History is all about change and conflict. It is not a comfortable subject.
The Isles: A History, Norman Davies 1999

Prehistoric cave, Moking Hurth

Prehistoric relics clearly show that the North Pennines have been occupied since before the time of written records. At *Moking Hurth* in Upper Teesdale, excavations have unearthed a Stone Age encampment from over 6000 years ago with the finds demonstrating the people then were opportunistic hunter-gatherers. Further evidence shows that the site was also occupied 3000 years ago and later about 2000 years ago, by which time rudimentary farming systems had been introduced (e.g. oat crops). Similar confirmation of long occupation exists from the *Heathery Burn* caves near Stanhope: the remarkable finds there included bronze swords, axes, spears, animal tools, gold and jet bracelets, and a bronze bucket (now in the British Museum). The Eden valley contains a series of stone circles, most notably *Long Meg and her Daughters* which seems to have been used by Neolithic people as a calendar. Seen from the centre of the circle, the midwinter sun sets directly over Long Meg and would have signalled the return of lengthening daylight again. In addition, at several locations on the Pennine moors are enigmatic cup-and-ring marked rocks. As farming developed, so the clearings in the forest became larger, and a period of major deforestation occurred from 2000BC-200AD.

The landscape changed with the arrival of the organisational and technical skills of the Romans. Local resistance was systematically subdued: the great earthwork ramparts at Stanwick camp (near Scotch Corner) indicate where the Brigantes of Venutius made an unsuccessful last stand against the invaders. The local inhabitants were then forced to accept the conditions of the *pax Romana*, but thereafter trade developed between natives and occupiers. The ancient route across Stainmore was upgraded into a strategic cross-Pennine road, and the Maiden Way constructed from the Eden valley to South Tynedale and the borderlands. In the east, Dere Street linked with York, whilst the Stanegate completed the network to the north. Major forts were built in strategic places such as at Bowes and Brough, with the border to the north eventually sealed by the monumental construction of Hadrian's Wall. At *Whitley Castle*, near Alston, the presence of a fort in an intriguingly remote location, strongly suggests the Romans used it as a base from which to control the output from the early mines. There are also traces of a Roman road across Eggleston Common which may be associated with a similar interest in the mines of Weardale.

During the so-called 'Dark Ages' following the withdrawal of the Romans, Anglian invaders began to establish a permanent presence north of the Humber (the land of 'Northumbria'). In general, these people preferred to settle the lowlands, choosing sheltered sites with well-drained ground suitable for arable land. As a result, the uplands of the North Pennines remained at the fringes of their influence, continuing to be very sparsely peopled by the Celtic natives (collectively referred to as 'Welsh' by the Angles).

Subsequently, Scandanavian invaders also began to settle in northern England. Danish people appeared from the east, expanding outwards from their occupation of York. From the 10th century onwards, Norse settlers begun to infiltrate the uplands from the west, moving from their original bases in Ireland and the Isle of Man through Cumbria and over the Pennines to the heads of the eastern dales. Although territorial control was an issue, few conflicts over land occurred because the Norse tended to occupy the uplands and valley-heads along with the scattered remnants of Celtic folk, whilst the Angles and Danes preferred the lowlands.

Hence, a different way of life became established in the uplands. In summer, settlers moved with their stock from the valleys to shielings on the fells, a pattern of *transhumance* that maximised the available pasturage. In Teesdale, relicts of old settlements on Holwick Fell have been noted to have many of the characteristics of those established by Norse colonies elsewhere, such as in the Faeroes and Iceland. These settlements were typically small and dispersed, scattered irregularly over the less productive uplands, by contrast to the Anglo-Danish communities of the lowlands which tended to be clustered, nucleated villages. Place-names provide a fascinating (if not completely reliable) insight into the origin of a settlement. Amongst many distinctions, Danish names are often characterised with a -*by* or -*thorp* suffix, Anglian names by -*ley*, -*ing* or -*ham*, and Norse names by -*thwaite* or -*gill*. Within the upland core, Norse descriptive names are widespread, *'fell'* and *'dale'* having become standard terms. However, *'hope'* which is typically used for an upland side-valley comes from an old Celtic word (*'hwpp'*). The Norse do not seem to have penetrated much further north and eastwards than the Eden Valley and Teesdale, leaving the other upper dales to be settled later; the boundary is clearly implied today by the transition of streams from *'beck'* to *'burn'*, ravines from *'gill'* to *'cleugh'*, and waterfalls from *'force'* to *'linn'*.

Organised early settlement of the dales was interrupted by the Norman conquest, during which insurrection in the north was ruthlessly quashed. A feudal system became established, with local overlords controlling village life from castles through service duty and *feu* payments. The Normans also developed their penchant for hunting by defining large restricted areas, such as at Geltsdale and Knarsdale, as deer forests for the privileged few. In Weardale, Stanhope and Wolsingham deer parks were controlled by the martial Prince Bishops of Durham as part of an autonomous County Palatine in which they had total authority.

Medieval settlements were typically surrounded by narrow strip plots ('tofts') with a plot of glebe land reserved for the church. In places, cultivation terraces facilitated the growing of crops: those at Eggleston (Teesdale) are amongst the best-preserved today. Related features are *lynchets*, ridge-and-furrow patterns marking the ploughing tracks used by oxen, either along the slope or occasionally up and down it. By the fast-flowing streams, mills utilised the water power to grind corn supplied by the local farms or imported from the more fertile lowlands.

The disruption and unrest following from the War of the Scottish Succession in the 14th century opened up much of northern England to raiders from across the border, and this would continue until the time of Union between the two crowns. However, not all the raiders were Scots: many of the notorious 'Border Reivers' and mosstroopers were opportunist pillagers from the turbulent lands of north Tynedale. This terrible scourge necessitated better defensive structures, and the result was a plethora of fortified buildings to protect both people and livestock.

Brough Castle: Norman fortress built upon site of Roman fort

In the Tyne valley, a chain of castles was constructed at Naworth, Blenkinsopp, Thirlwall, Bellister and Featherstone. The Allendales were protected by Langley Castle and Staward Pele together with the fortification of Burnlaw Hall. Further east, typically guarding river fords, were the castles at Beaufront, Aydon, Halton, Bywell and Prudhoe. Another favoured raiders' route was by the Vale of Eden and Stainmore, hence the series of castles built at Dacre, Penrith, Brougham, Kirkoswald, Appleby, Brough, Augill, Harley, Lammerside and Pendragon. Similarly to the east of Stainmore, castles existed at Barnard Castle, Bowes, Cotherstone, Scargill, Streatlam, Brancepeth, Witton, Raby and Ravensworth.

Castles were built only by the most powerful and richest overlords. Other lesser nobles built fortified tower houses known as *peles (or peels)*, thick-walled structures with two or three upper floors above a basement that was used to stock provisions and guarded by a heavy iron-studded door. Notable examples surviving today include those at Ninebanks, Staward Pele, Willimoteswick, Randoldholme, Mortham Tower and Howgill Castle. Meanwhile, farmers in the uplands built defensive farmhouses *(bastles)*, with an onus on retaining livestock: many good examples also remain of these buildings, especially in Allendale and Weardale.

Egglestone Abbey

Granting of land from beneficial landowners also enabled the establishment of monasteries which then developed into major landowners in themselves. In the North Pennines, the White Canons of the Premonstratensian Order established abbeys at both Egglestone and Blanchland, whilst the Augustinian Order had a major base at Hexham. In the north-west, a priory was established at Wetheral by the Benedictine Abbey of York. The most successful establishments had many business interests, including metalworking and farming, often with large sheep flocks on an extensive pasturage.

The earliest mining records date from medieval times, although undoubtedly there were operations that pre-dated this. These early workings would have been based upon stream deposits or used shallow line-shafts to access mineral veins. Hand-operated *jack rollers* for winding up material to the surface in kebbles evolved into the use of deeper *whimsey* shafts using a horse gin that circumscribed a circular path around the shaft top. Alston Moor was worked under a Royal lease and supplied the 'Silver Mines of Carlisle', linked to the establishment of a mint in that city. Miners and ancillary workers (e.g. smelters) were conscripted and in return had certain privileges, notably the right to cut timber. An influx of people into some of the other valley heads at this time may also relate to mining interests, such as the planned settlements that the Bishop of Durham developed in Weardale.

As the scourge of the Border raids finally declined, so trade began to flourish. Following the lifting of cross-border restrictions in 1611 and tolls in 1672, an important market developed for Scottish cattle to be driven south from trysts at Falkirk and Crieff, fattened, and then sold at large fairs. The drovers established a system of routes that avoided towns and cultivated land on the lowlands by crossing the moors and fells, leading to broad 'green ways' across the uplands. One of the main southbound drovers' routes was via Gilsland, from where the track crossed the moors to join the Maiden Way up South Tynedale past Alston. Two branches diverged at Alston: one route continued on the Maiden Way over the Pennine watershed to Kirkland, then travelled through the Vale of Eden to Brough Hill Fair, Kirkby Stephen and the markets of the south. The other branch continued up South Tynedale, crossed to the Tees at Moor House, then followed a track via Birkdale and Cronkley Fell to Holwick, before crossing the moors to the Greta at God's Bridge. A completely alternative route went further east, via Blanchland and Stanhope to Eggleston, eventually joining the route previously described or continuing via Barnard Castle to Richmond and Thirsk. At its peak, large numbers of cattle were driven south: by the mid-18th century it is estimated 80,000 passed through the Eden valley annually. However, when the more efficient railways arrived in the 19th century, cattle droving declined.

Another boom from the 17th century onwards, was the practice of enclosure. Parliamentary Enclosure Acts allowed landowners to annex common land and then 'improve' it by raising agricultural productivity. Enclosure gradually extended from the valleys onto the uplands: Knarsdale Common was one of the last areas to be enclosed in 1859. An important constituent of the 'improvement' process was lime applied to the soil to counter its acidity, hence, the profusion of kilns for processing locally quarried limestone. In Weardale, encouraged by the Bishop of Durham, over 60,000 acres had been enclosed by 1800, causing considerable resentment amongst many of the local people who lost their traditional common land. During the Industrial Revolution, towns also often developed specialised industries associated with their local produce: Barnard Castle, for example, became known for dyeing and weaving products that were extracted from the coarser wools, including carpets.

Limekilns at Bishopley, Bollihope valley

Although worked for many centuries previously, the rich mineral deposits of the North Pennines were mined on a large-scale during the 18th and 19th century. The main ore was lead (principally *galena* but also some *cerrusite* or 'white lead'), although in the 20th century the previous waste *(gangue)* minerals of barytes and fluorspar also developed an economic value. Some locations also had a high silver yield, and zinc ore (*sphalerite*, 'blende' or 'blackjack') was recovered on a commercial scale at Nenthead and West Allendale.

The main businesses were run by the Blackett-Beaumonts (later known as WB Lead) and the London Lead Company, but there were also an array of smaller operators. The Blackett-Beaumont business began with Newcastle merchant William Blackett and continued as a family operation to run many mines in Allendale and Weardale. By contrast, the London Lead Company was a group of businessmen who developed mining on a large-scale at Alston Moor and in Teesdale, with less extensive workings in the Eden and Derwent valleys. Whilst the Blackett-Beaumont family owned much of the land from which they extracted minerals (although the Bishop of Durham had control in Weardale), the London Lead Company was a major lessee. Ownership of a large section of the northern dales, including Alston Moor, had been granted to the Commissioners of Greenwich Hospital after the confiscation of land from the pro-Jacobite Earl of Derwentwater. Both of these companies built housing for their workers, notably at Nenthead, Allenheads and Middleton. The directors of the London Lead Company were heavily influenced by their Quaker religion, and their developments are particularly noted for their emphasis on workers' education and welfare.

Mining was an arduous and hazardous occupation. Working lives were short, with tuberculosis and dust-induced silicosis being the main killers. The early method of working the veins via shafts or open-cuts *(rakes)* was superseded by the use of levels, which were driven both for ease of access (horse levels) and as drainage systems (wet levels). Cross-cuts from the levels were used to intercept adjacent veins, with shafts used for ventilation and as quick routes to the surface. Two of the levels were major achievements for their time: Nentforce Level on Alston Moor and the Blackett Level in East Allendale. The old method of *'hushing'* continued to be used, however, to both prospect for and facilitate working of veins. 'Hushes' were created by the abrupt release of water from an upslope reservoir along a prepared trench to scour and remove debris, eventually scouring a deep channel through repeated releases. Smaller 'hushes' were also used to wash mine wastes as small amounts of the heavier ore were left behind as a residue.

Exploration was inevitably a mixture of skill and luck. Promising veins were frequently abandoned on discovering little ore, or because the 'Old Man' had already worked-out the vein. Miners were employed in teams under a piecework 'bargain' system, each contract reflecting either current prospects for mining a vein *(bingtale)* or driving a level *(fathomtale)*. A fixed monthly advance or 'lent' was provided by the company for subsistence. The lent had to be repaid on closing the contract; in the event of a 'bad bargain', the debt remained and the miner found himself 'in the Master's books'. As many of the mines were some distance from workers' homes, crude accommodation was provided in lodging *'shops'*, with the miner returning home at the weekend. These 'shops' were poorly-ventilated and usually severely overcrowded, often housing 30-40 men in one small building, meaning any disease could easily spread. Very few of the working miners were aged over 40 and not many lived beyond 50.

Once the lead ore ('bouse') had been hacked from the veins, it was transported to stone storage hoppers in the *bousesteems*, one for each mining team. The bouse was then 'dressed' to remove the lighter waste from the heavy galena, by crushing it and then progressively grading and separating out the heavier ore; often this work was done by children. Later, crushing mills with water-driven rollers were introduced to alleviate the manual effort involved in breaking down the rock. The processed ore ('bing') was then taken to the smelter, where it was heated in a large hearth fired by coal or peat, typically with a bellows driven by power from a water-wheel. The heat drove off impurities as gas, and the molten metal could then be tapped into moulds to form lead 'pigs'. Waste gases were further smelted in a slag hearth to extract more lead. In the early 19th century, with the development of the reverberatory furnace allowing a better cleaner product, long chimney flues appeared. The chimneys removed poisonous fumes to a distant outlet but also had the dual benefit of allowing recovery of more of the precious lead which would accumulate as a coating within the flue, to be removed by worker boys. The location of many smelters at some distance from the mines is an indication of the importance of a good coal supply. Water power was also vital for crushing, dressing and smelting, therefore supplied by elaborate systems of water leats and reservoirs.

'Dry' level, with trace of the old wooden rails, Great Rundale.

'Wet' level, for mine drainage: the famous Blackett Level, Allendale.

Before the advent of the railways, packhorse routes were the major means of transport. Some of these 'galloway trods' or 'jagger lanes' are still evident today on the moors, such as the Broad Way and Carriers' Way above Allendale. Similarly, 'salt roads' (e.g. at Salter's Gate, near Wolsingham) were used to distribute salt from the coastal estuaries, which was in demand for preserving meat. In the 19th century, there was considerable investment in roads, with toll-gated turnpikes gradually replacing the maintenance of tracks by local parishes. The mining companies also built new roads, especially over the fells, and many of the higher fell roads date from this time. One of their main contractors, John McAdam introduced his 'tarmac' innovation to bind together the roadstone and prevent it being washed away.

An important part of the miners' existence was to take a smallholding at the fringes of the existing cultivated area. This has been appropriately described as 'three acres and a pig', although a cow could also be kept, and sheep would be pastured on the adjacent moor. The mining companies encouraged this activity: as well as the health benefits, it could also bring in extra money as rent! In some cases, as with the London Lead Company, assistance was actually given to the miners in building cottages to work this marginal land. Most of these holdings have now been abandoned and the land partly reverted back to rough pasture, although still clearly recognisable by its ruined buildings and walled enclosures. The miners also developed a strong interest in education, probably because with the bargain system they were working for themselves and knowledge became a valuable asset. Interest in the local rocks extended to building elaborate *spar boxes* containing displays of the best crystals they had found.

The mining industry collapsed at the end of the 19th century when the arrival of cheaper imports drastically lowered the price of lead. The resulting loss of work led to substantial depopulation with people moving east to the coalfield area or even emigrating overseas. The London Lead Company was wound up in 1905, and mining operations generally passed to smaller ephemeral companies, or specialist operators such as Vieille Montagne (from Belgium). Barytes became an important mineral because of its many economic uses, notably as a drilling fluid (in demand again with the development of North Sea oil in the 1960s). Fluorspar also had an economic value, both as a flux in steel-making and more recently in the chemical industry. For a while, during the 1960s and 1970s, many of those local people who owned tractors were supplementing their income by foraging the old mine waste dumps for fluorspar deposits!

Although quarrying was developed in other areas, in Weardale it has been a major industry for many centuries. Trade expanded from the extraction of 'Frosterley marble' into the massive limestone quarries that supplied both the steelworks of the coalfield and the local cement works at Eastgate. Commercial mining of iron ore has also been extensive in the same valley following the founding

Human History

of the Weardale Iron Company in 1845. To transport materials, a remarkably ambitious and technically advanced mineral railway system was built over the fells using long inclines and winding engines, linking Stanhope, Rookhope and Westgate with their markets. Only at a later stage was this superseded by a valley railway, whilst during the same period, steelworks were built at Wolsingham and Stanhope.

The often harsh conditions of the upland valleys proved a fertile ground for the Methodist religion. The Quakers also developed a small local presence in some areas, with meeting houses at Alston, Coanwood, Allendale Town and Cotherstone. In each case, developments tended to be a reaction against the rigid hierarchy of the established Church. In upper Weardale and around Alston, there is some evidence to suggest that a small band of Scottish Convenanters found sanctuary there, and Presbyterianism was certainly active in pockets before Methodism took over. Groups of 'independents' also sprung up, such as the Inghamites who once had a presence in the Eden valley, but were again mainly drawn into Methodism. Many villages have two types of Methodist chapel, a Wesleyian version and a Primitive (or 'ranters') chapel, after a split over doctrine in the 19th century. The mining companies encouraged religion and other organised activities such as reading, study and formation of musical bands. Co-operative societies also flourished to encourage local self-sufficiency.

Other land uses began to become important from the late 19th century. As water supply for growing towns became an issue, large reservoirs were built in some of the upland valleys. Meanwhile, on the grouse moors, large sporting estates became established with local employment and infrastructure based upon maintaining effective numbers of game birds, despite natural cyclic fluctuations. In the 20th century, with the formation of the Forestry Commission, sections of moorland were planted for commercial forestry, notably at Hamsterley and Slaley, east of the Pennines.

Farming has continued to be the mainstay of the local economy, with dairy and beef cattle on the lower farms, and sheep on the hill farms. In the enclosed in-bye pastures, soils have been improved by application of lime and the grazing quality regularly boosted by the application of nitrogen and phosphorous from fertiliser or manure. As a result, cultivation has reached high into the uplands, at elevations up to 550m, and beyond this sheep can roam the high fells. Field barns (laithes) to store hay and provide winter shelter for livestock remain a prominent feature of the landscape. Key events in the hill-farming calendar are lambing at springtime and the making of silage or hay during the summer, with the traditional agricultural shows still remaining an important focal point of dales' life.

End of an era: demolition of Eastgate cement works chimney in 2005

Snow drifts on Scurreth Edge

Stainmore and Upper Eden

Here begins that mountainous and vast tract, always exposed to wind and rain,
which from its being rough and stony is called by the inhabitants Stonemore
Britannica, William Camden 1590

Stainmore marks the upland transition between the Yorkshire Dales and the North Pennines, forming a broad depression in the hills which provides a major east-west trans-Pennine crossing. However, most of it is generally unfrequented territory providing a land of unexpected surprises with a fascinating history. The administrative district of Stainmore is on the western approaches above the Eden valley, and for our purposes the geographical limits have been extended in this direction to include Kirkby Stephen and the Nine Standards. This may be topographically inexact but the Nine Standards do have a clear association with the Stainmore district and the extension concurs with the boundaries of the North Pennines AONB.

The pass of Stainmore has been a key route through the Pennines since prehistoric times. Since then, a constant stream of travellers have come this way including Roman legions, Scandanavian settlers, packhorse traders, marching armies, cattle drovers and stage-coach passengers. Now the car and juggernaut prevail, but despite the advances made by modern engineering in building the A66 highway, the route retains its reputation for snow, wind and fog. In times past it was frequently a difficult, even dangerous, crossing.

The Pennine crossing has historically represented the crucial link in the main route between the cities of York and Carlisle. Its strategic importance meant that the Romans built one of their military roads over the pass with a station on the summit at Maiden Castle and forts at either end (Brough and Bowes) to maintain control. The earthwork ramparts at Maiden Castle remain today, together with the platforms used for signal stations at higher points on the moor. During medieval times, a series of hospices *('spittals')* were established with support from the monasteries to provide sustenance and shelter for weary travellers; some of these buildings still remain today. A Moor Guide was also available to assist wayfarers. In 1743 the route became a turnpike, with the villages of Brough and Bowes on either side of the crossing becoming important coaching centres. Compared to the modern road, the old way between Stainmore summit and Brough was steeper but provided more shelter from the potentially severe conditions on the moors.

To the east of Stainmore summit is the ancient monument of Rey Cross, by tradition marking the site where Erik Bloodaxe, last Viking ruler of York and exiled former king of Norway (son of Harold Fine-hair), was killed during a skirmish with rivals in 954AD. Thereafter, until the late 11th century, the pass was the boundary between the lands of Northumbria and Strathclyde, effectively making it the border between the nascent countries of England and Scotland. A 17th century chronicler records the coats-of-arms of the two countries on either side of Rey Cross, but these have now gone and only the shaft of the cross remains (it was also moved slightly during the A66 upgrade works). Until 1974, the boundary then separated the counties of Westmorland and Yorkshire, but since that time the demarcation has been between Cumbria and County Durham. Rather curiously, the county boundary line in this vicinity does not follow the watershed but keeps just to the east of it by a series of straight-line segments between isolated marker stones; this was apparently the outcome of an investigation by the Tithe Commissioners after a dispute over the exact line had occurred.

A rail link over the pass came in 1861, when the South Durham & Lancashire Union Railway established the route for transporting Durham coke to the ironworks of Furness (now in south Cumbria). A side-effect of this development was also to boost the movement of people from the North-East to Blackpool on holiday! As may be expected, the line was often blocked by snow, occasionally for several weeks, with large teams of snow-cutters required to re-excavate the line through the drifts. The station at Barras, just to the west of the summit of the pass, was then the highest in the country with a prospect of the Eden valley considered by many to be amongst the best in the land from a railway line. To the west, a magnificent iron-girder viaduct was constructed to carry the line in a sweeping curve around and above the Belah valley (where the old signal box still remains but the viaduct has unfortunately long gone from the scene) then continuing onwards to Kirby Stephen. A steady post-war decline in business and a harsh economic climate meant that the line eventually closed in 1960, with much of the infrastructure removed very quickly thereafter.

South Stainmore, in late summer, from Hardhills

For a traveller crossing over Stainmore pass, the abrupt transition between the bleak swarthy Pennine moors and the verdant pastures of the Eden valley remains a distinctive physical threshold. Often this is accompanied by a change in the weather: from fog on the moor to sun in the valley; or, during a temperature inversion, from a bright clear hillside into dense freezing fog that lingers in the valley. At other times, fingers of *haar* cloud can stretch out from the North Sea to shroud the eastern slopes, only to dissipate in the bright sunshine and warmth of the Eden valley-side. Frequently conditions can rapidly deteriorate on the approaches to the pass, with the featureless moor lost in thick fog or enveloped by great plumes of snow and spindrift drifting wildly in the unfettered wind.

A notable landmark set amongst the bleak moors to the south of Stainmore is *Tan Hill Inn*. This historic staging post is the highest inn in the country, and has long acted as a focal point for old roads and tracks that link the Eden valley, Teesdale, Swaledale and Arkengarthdale. On a clear day, the panorama is archetypal Pennine, vast rolling moorland extending north across Stainmore Common to the prominent whaleback rise of Mickle Fell. In the past, drovers and farmers would converge at Tan Hill for meets, trade and sustenance. Coal was mined from an extensive series of local pits on the adjacent slopes and transported along the roads to the villages, halls and castles in the nearby valleys. For a brief period of time, following the 1974 boundary re-organisation, Tan Hill Inn moved from Yorkshire to County Durham but the expense of clearing snowdrifts to take its younger inhabitants to school meant administrative control soon returned to North Yorkshire by a subtle modification of the boundary line.

Tan Hill Inn

The Cumbrian district of Stainmore lies on the Eden flanks of the pass, where a fertile green bowl scattered with occasional farmsteads contrasts with the desolate ochre moors. The scene is particularly well revealed from high viewpoints to the south, such as at Barras or from the prominent stone pillars of the Nine Standards. In winter and spring, snow-drifts often linger on the fellsides and in sheltered nooks.

The scattering of isolated farmsteads making up both North and South Stainmore are indicative of the typical mode of settlement of the Scandanavian settlers who first made their homes here. Bell-pits and ruined mine buildings (including a former smelt mill at Augill) indicate where exploration for coal and minerals (lead and copper) occurred, but there were no major finds to compare with developments elsewhere in the North Pennines. Similarly, high up on the moors at Slate Quarry Moss and High Greygrits, flagstones were quarried: of inadequate quality for export, they nevertheless provided abundant material for roofing the local houses.

North Stainmore

A distinctive feature of the Stainmore district is that the streams have often incised deep ravines where they descend towards the main valley floor. These gorges are typically hidden from obvious view, but contain exquisite woodlands encouraging a diverse range of flora and fauna. Formerly, elm wychwoods flourished here but disease has left the trees as dying, dead or rotting hulks, slowly being recycled into new living material. However, ash continues to thrive in these secluded hollows, and together with other species such as hazel and birch, provides a very attractive setting for those wishing to explore their secretive recesses.

In the vicinity of North Stainmore, notable gorges occur at both Swindale and Augill. Swindale is the deepest of the valleys and also the most conspicuous, being easily accessed from Brough. By contrast, Augill is something of a surprise, the Borrowdale Beck falling abruptly into an enclosed ravine scarcely suspected from the A66 despite the lofty viaduct by which it crosses the valley. Nearby, Augill Castle is a rather grandiose Victorian mansion, built in 1842, and adorned with a series of castellated turrets.

Similarly, near South Stainmore, Argill Beck falls over a series of limestone steps into a gorge amidst beautiful woodland. The section between Gillbank and Low Dowgill has been set aside as a nature reserve, and is accompanied by a charming stream-side path. To the south, near Barras, is another sharp ravine at Mouse Gill. Barras takes its name from the original version of 'Barhouse' indicating that there was originally a toll-gate here. Its elevated situation also overlooks the beautiful Belah valley where gurgling streams descend from the desolate moors to a sparkling river that turns a rich creamy-brown in spate. Here are further wooded gorges and fine cascades, with a network of paths leading to the upper reached beyond Ewebank and Wrenside that are well worth exploring. Lower down are the quiet villages of Kaber and Winton, the latter with an attractive old corn mill by a small tributary stream. A little further south is Hartley village, particularly attractively arranged along a long green either side of another lively stream.

The deep wooded valley of Swindale

Hartley village

> 'Ash-Boughs'
> Not of ál my eyes see, wandering on the world,
> Is anything a milk to the mind, so sighs deep
> Poetry tó it, as a tree whose boughs break in the sky.
> Say it is ásh-boughs: whether on December day and furled
> Fast ór they in clammyish lashtender combs creep
> Apart wide and new-nestle at heaven most high.
>   Gerard Manley Hopkins

The skyline profile of the Nine Standards

The main settlement in the upper Eden valley is *Kirkby Stephen*, an old market town that gained from its key position on important trading routes. The town gained its first market charter in 1351 with a speciality being the production and trade of woollen stockings. Pillared cloisters on the north side of the market indicate the entrance to the large parish church of St. Stephen, and were formerly used to store butter for the market. The link between the town's name and the patron saint of the church is not as clear as may be thought, most authorities suggesting that in fact the name is corrupted from 'Kirkby on t'Eden', consistent with other descriptive 'Kirkby' place-names elsewhere. A distinctive feature of the town is the local rock used in many of the buildings. This is *brockram*, consisting of limestone fragments cemented within a pink sandstone matrix, a result of rapid deposition of eroded material without time for settling or sorting.

At the southern end of the town, the River Eden flows through a spectacular narrow gorge at Stenkrith. The waters have eroded the brockram into a series of fissures, potholes and caverns, with foaming cauldrons and sinister eddies. The larger potholes have formed pools or 'dubs', where the waters have swirled pebbles around in the constrictions, notably at Cowkarney Hole under the bridge. Deep rumblings from subterranean passages sound like the crushing and grinding of machinery, hence the local name of the *'The Devil's Mustard Mill'*.

The Nine Standards

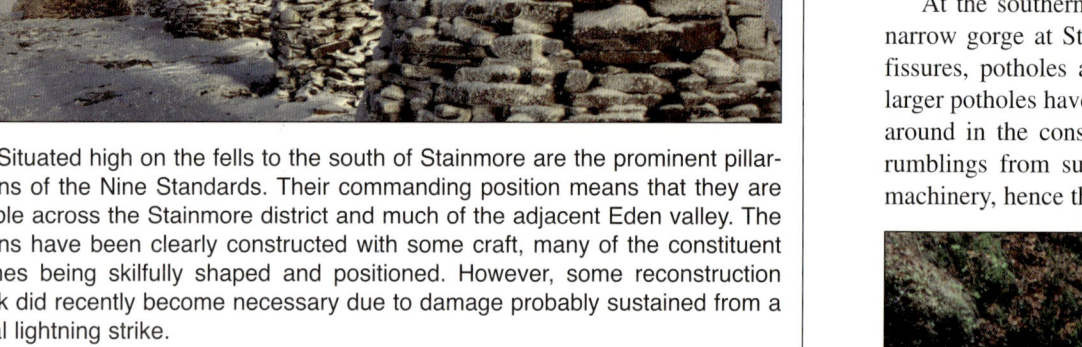

Situated high on the fells to the south of Stainmore are the prominent pillar-cairns of the Nine Standards. Their commanding position means that they are visible across the Stainmore district and much of the adjacent Eden valley. The cairns have been clearly constructed with some craft, many of the constituent stones being skilfully shaped and positioned. However, some reconstruction work did recently become necessary due to damage probably sustained from a local lightning strike.

The Standards have a long history, being marked on 18th century maps and mentioned in Sir Walter Scott's poem *'The Bridal of Triermain'*. Various suggestions have been made on why they were built, the real reason having been lost to history. Amongst the most fanciful is the conjecture that their prominent position was intended to discourage Scottish invaders by suggesting an encamped army. An alternative theory is that they are built to mark a boundary, although the present county line now turns east further south. A sounder supposition is that they resulted from local customs or rivalry; the position certainly provides an expansive 'shop-window' for the structures. Key clues to their origin seems to be given by their orientation, all in a straight line, and of course, by the magnificent location near the summit of Nine Standards Rigg, providing a sumptuous view across Stainmore and the Eden valley backed by the Pennine escarpment, with Mickle Fell and Cross Fell prominent. This suggests that the hill was also probably a beacon site with flames lit to warn the upper Eden valley of invaders or during major celebrations. Approach can be made from the Hartley Fell road or Lambs Moss (B6270).

Devil's Mustard Mill, Stenkrith (see also p.10)

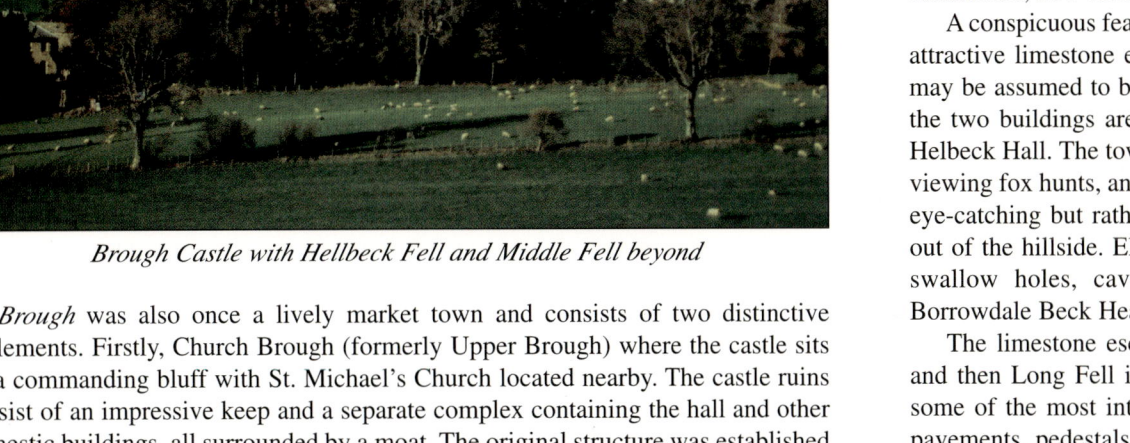
Brough Castle with Hellbeck Fell and Middle Fell beyond

Brough was also once a lively market town and consists of two distinctive settlements. Firstly, Church Brough (formerly Upper Brough) where the castle sits on a commanding bluff with St. Michael's Church located nearby. The castle ruins consist of an impressive keep and a separate complex containing the hall and other domestic buildings, all surrounded by a moat. The original structure was established in the 11th century on the site of the Roman fort of *Verterae*, the earthworks of which can be seen in the adjacent field. Subsequent rebuilding became necessary after a raid by the Scots in 1174. As a baronry fortress for the Clifford family, it was a property of the ruthless 'Bloody Clifford' who appears in Shakespeare's 'Henry VI' as a supporter of the Lancastrian cause during the Wars of the Roses. The castle then fell into ruin after a fire but was subsequently rebuilt in the 17th century by Lady Anne Clifford who did much restoration work in the area (see p.32). Unfortunately, another fire thereafter and the lure of good stone, some being used for Appleby Castle, meant that it was progressively dismantled.

The so-called Market Place located in the street leading to the castle and church has been re-built from its original position on the Kirkby Stephen road. It was originally intended that this would be an important trading centre, but the rival settlement of Market Brough (formerly Low Brough) located on the old Stainmore-Appleby road usurped this role and has since developed as the main settlement. Brough reached its heyday during the days of the stage-coach, when all available accommodation was often crammed full with weary travellers. The route over the Pennines was operated by two regular coaches, the Express and the Glasgow Mail, joined for a short time by a third, The Herald. Such were the difficulties experienced on the crossing of Stainmore that damaged or overturned coaches were not uncommon. Now, however, life at Brough is much less hectic. Traffic on the A66 highway is busier than ever, but the bypass means that it roars past the village without the need to stop. The famous Brough Hill Fair, an autumnal complement to the early summer meet at Appleby and once a major cattle exchange, is also rather diminished, now lasting only a day.

A conspicuous feature from Brough is the cylindrical Fox's Tower situated on an attractive limestone escarpment above the fine ashwoods of Helbeck Wood. This may be assumed to be a mining relic, looking almost like a smelting chimney, but the two buildings are in fact a 'folly' built in 1775 by John Metcalf Carleton of Helbeck Hall. The tower is said to have been constructed to provide a beldevere for viewing fox hunts, and has a spiral staircase and lunch room with fireplace. Another eye-catching but rather less aesthetic feature is the huge limestone quarry clawed out of the hillside. Elsewhere the limestone band has produced a series of hidden swallow holes, caves and springs above North Stainmore extending from Borrowdale Beck Head to the Jingle Holes and Swindale Head.

The limestone escarpment continues north-west from Helbeck to Middle Fell and then Long Fell in a series of gently-folded craggy bluffs. This area contains some of the most interesting limestone features in the North Pennines, including pavements, pedestals and dry valleys. Sections of the pavements show the classic pattern of weathered 'clints' that are cut by deep 'grykes' harbouring a range of exotic flora in their recesses. Unfortunately, large parts of this attractive landscape are located within the MOD Warcop Range which is regularly used for live firing, and therefore has restricted access. However, for adventurous souls, limited access is possible along rights-of-way on certain non-firing days, although great care needs to be taken to avoid any old shells. The level of exclusion within the Range is regrettable, but the situation has been improving in recent years and the army do undertake important conservation work to protect vulnerable habitats.

Sheltering below the escarpment is *Warcop*, one of the most attractive villages in Cumbria. At the quaint church of St. Columba, the annual rush-bearing ceremony is still held every St. Peter's Day (29th June), commemorating the times when the wet clay floors of churches needed to be covered with rushes every year. A similar festival is held at St. Theobald's in the nearby village of Great Musgrave (traditionally, the first Saturday of July). Equally picturesque is the 16th century Warcop Bridge over the River Eden. In springtime, the profusion of cherry trees around Warcop marks the season with a vibrant display of blossom.

Jingle Holes

Limestone Landscapes

If it form the one landscape that we, the inconstant ones,
Are consistently homesick for, this is chiefly
Because it dissolves in water. Mark these rounded slopes
With their surface fragrance of thyme and, beneath,
A secret system of caves and conduits;
In Praise of Limestone, WH Auden

Limestone is a rather special rock. Despite its hardness, it has an inherent chemical weakness for rain-water which dissolves it into a fascinating array of peculiar forms: shakeholes, swallow-holes, caverns, fissures, pavements and flutes. Plants love it too, and outcrops are typically characterised by a green and lush landscape, often featuring exotic species, contrasting with the surrounding moorland. The North Pennines do not quite have the remarkable diversity of solution (karst) features as the Craven district of Yorkshire or the Burren in Ireland because the limestone beds are thinner. However, in certain places, such as on Helbeck Fell, the same distinctive landscape is found with all its myriad attractions. It should be doubly cherished: demands from industry and for use in gardens has meant that quarrying has removed much of this valuable scenery throughout the country, including the vast majority of the limestone pavements.

Limestone rocks on Hellbeck Fell

Helbeck Fell

Looking over the East Fellside, from Murton Pike

Eden and East Fellside

To meet the Atlantic's boundless time,
See old Ituna's waters glide,
As rolls the river to the sea,
So time until eternity.

William Mounsey [19th century inscription: Constantine's Cells, Wetheral]

The Eden is the main river on the west side of the North Pennines, rising on Mallerstang Edge and then flowing unerringly north-west towards the Solway Firth near Carlisle. Although an Anglo-Saxon derivation for its name has been suggested, a Celtic origin seems much more likely, especially as '-don' is a commonly used component of river-names throughout Europe. Similarly, the Romans seem to have used this literal root in naming the river as 'Ituna'. Those that have suggested a possible Biblical inspiration in the name may have been guided more by the beautiful landscape through which the river flows rather than historical precedent!

The geographical district described in this chapter may appropriately be termed 'East of Eden'. Below Kirkby Stephen the river flows across a broad fertile vale which is bounded on its eastern edge by the bold feature of the Pennine escarpment, where steep slopes rise abruptly up to the high fells. The transition between valley floor and fell is the land of the *East Fellside*, marking the zone where the lush valley pastures merge into the rougher steeper ground of the hills. Beyond this transition, the highest of the Pennines rise in a continuous wall and are clearly visible in favourable conditions throughout the entire Eden valley. Cross Fell is pre-eminent, not only as the highest of the range but also dominating the scene through its sheer bulk. At intervals, deep side-valleys cut through the escarpment, enhancing the diversity and contrast; on this side of the Pennines, these short valleys are known as 'dales'.

On the lowlands, a few miles away from the fells, is the ancient borough town of *Appleby* set in a sheltered location by a particularly attractive loop of the River Eden. Formerly the administrative centre of the old county of Westmorland and with a Royal Charter dating back to 1179, the town had to endure much rebuilding during the time of the Border raiders when the fertile lowlands of the Eden valley became a favourite target. The restored Norman castle keep is located at the top of the Boroughgate, a broad central avenue rising between the twin obelisks of Low Cross and High Cross bordered by fine Georgian or Victorian buildings and the 16th century Moot Hall. Both the castle and town are indelibly associated with the remarkable life of Lady Anne Clifford, who was a major influence throughout Westmorland (p.32). However, Appleby is probably most widely known for its annual Horsefair, held every June. During the time of the fair, gypsy folk and other country people from all over northern England (and further afield) converge upon the town to generate a rather distinctive carnival atmosphere.

Boroughgate, Appleby

> ### Lady Anne Clifford
>
> Born in 1590 as daughter of Lord Clifford, Earl of Cumberland, Lady Anne had an extraordinary life. Despite being of small stature (4ft 10in or 1.47m), she was of strong spirit and indomitable will, and became widely renowned for her charitable nature. Twice unhappily married, she eventually inherited the Clifford family estates in Westmorland and Yorkshire in 1643 after many years of legal wrangling. The inheritance included six castles in various stages of ruin, amongst which were those at Appleby, Brough and Pendragon in the Eden valley. Also included in the legacy was the important role of High Sheriff of Westmorland.
>
> During her years in power, Lady Anne restored all of the castles, spending time at each of them in turn, and she also rescued many other derelict buildings from ruin. Every Monday, she would distribute ten shillings to twenty of the poorest local people and would also insist on buying her household requirements locally. In Appleby, she transformed St. Lawrence's Church, restored the almshouses and re-built St. Michael's Church. When she died at the age of eighty six, an exceptionally old age for those times, she was interred in a grand tomb at Appleby St. Lawrence's.

The East Fellside is characterised by a series of attractive villages, each sturdily built from the reddish Eden sandstone, and nestling close to or at the foot of the hills. The sunny aspect and warm building stone enhances their charm, bringing an inviting glow to the houses as the westering sun declines towards sunset. Another feature is the often tight enclosure of buildings around the village green, particularly well-displayed at Milburn. This is a defensive relic from the times when Border raids were frequent, but it now gives the villages a particular identity. The seemingly idyllic setting of the East Fellside does, however, have a downside which despite being open knowledge, continues to literally 'bowl over' the unwary! This is the harsh and volatile force of the *Helm Wind* (p.40), a severe weather phenomenon blasting down from the fells. During its meteorological extremes, outdoor life in the villages and farms becomes a continuous struggle, with the sturdy buildings themselves strongly tested amid an over-riding necessity to 'batten down the hatches'.

The steep slopes of the East Fellside also provide a clear exhibition of the distinctive geology of the Pennine escarpment. Breaking the regular sweep of the escarpment as it rise from valley-floor to fell-top is a series of very prominent lower hills, with distinctive peaked shapes that contrast with the flatter profiles of the higher fells. Most distinctive of these hills are the trio of Murton Pike, Dufton Pike and Knock Pike, although in fact they are contiguous with several other knobs and bumps, gradually rising in height to the south.

Murton Pike from Keisley

> ### The Pikes and the Cross Fell Inlier
>
> The prominent conical hills of the Pikes have been likened to sentinels overlooking the eastern fringes of the Eden valley. They are also frequently described as 'outliers' of the main fells, standing apart from the main massif.
>
> In geographical terms, they are certainly aptly described as outliers, but in geological terms they belong to the Cross Fell Inlier. By being termed an 'inlier' they are recognised as providing an anomalous exposure of older rocks completely surrounded by younger rocks. In this case, their presence can be attributed to the large-scale faulting on the Pennine escarpment that has thrown upwards an older group of rocks between the Eden valley and the high fells. In many regards, the shapely outlines of the Pikes have more of a similarity with the Lakeland Fells than the normal flat-topped Pennines, and they share an equivalent age and origin with the Lakeland rocks. As a result, the Inlier consists of slates and volcanic rocks squeezed in a narrow zone between the desert sandstones of the Eden valley and the shales, sandstones, limestones and gritstones of the higher fells.

Beyond the intervening rocks of the Pikes, the main slope of the escarpment provides an almost vertical cross-section through the rocks of the Alston Block, in places exposing the Whin Sill and several important mineral veins (see photo p.11). This providence was exploited by the miners, and as a result the slopes above the East Fellside have been pitted and scoured at key sites, especially in Scordale and on Dufton Fell. At the peak of the mining activity, the fellside villages were transformed by an influx of workers, but now they have once again returned to the quiet farming scene established since the time of the earliest settlers.

The most intensively mined area was above the twin villages of *Hilton* and *Murton*. Both villages are spiritually served by the tiny St. John's Church located midway between them, a pairing arrangement that is common on the East Fellside. Near to the bridge in Murton is the building that once housed a wood-turning mill, producing bobbins to supply the large demand from the spinning and weaving industries. When mining expanded in the 18th century, the London Lead Company became the main business, employing a large proportion of the inhabitants in both villages.

Cutting deeply into the hills is the valley of Scordale, forming a major break in the escarpment between the bold nose of Roman Fell and the broader mass of Murton Fell. Access to Scordale is rather limited as it is within the restricted military zone of the Warcop Range, as indicated by the rather discouraging warning notices. However, there is an old right-of-way through the valley which can be used on non-firing days. It provides a great scenic highlight, penetrating deep into the fells to become enclosed by extensive scree slopes and limestone crags.

The lowest mine building in Scordale was the former smelt mill, with the deep gash of Lowfield Hush prominent on the northern slopes opposite to the short hidden valley of Swindale. The use of 'hushing' to expose and work veins seems to have been particularly common on the slopes above the East Fellside; one large release of water at the White Mines above Murton was recorded as causing especially severe pollution to both the Trout Beck and the Eden in 1759.

The mine track in Scordale leads to extensive workings at Amber Hill and Dow Scar, where you may (if lucky!) find some of the amber-coloured 'barley-sugar' fluorspar cubes for which this area is renowned amongst mineralogists, or more likely the distinctive white platy crystals of barytes. High above, on the northern slopes, are the debris-strewn Mason Holes, which were apparently worked in medieval times. When lead mining ceased in the 1880s, barytes continued to be worked from the mines and spoil heaps until the 1950s. Beyond the upper mines, the valley walls close in completely and the main stream cascades down in waterfalls past more ruins and the remains of the dams used for water power. The track up to the head of the valley is rough but passable, vestiges of the old route that formerly passed this way over to the desolation of Maize Beck, thereby crossing the fells to Upper Teesdale (notwithstanding the potentially treacherous stream crossing involved).

A stormy day in Scordale

The next village to the north is *Dufton*, first settled by the Anglo-Danes who had founded nearby Appleby. The parish church is shared with the nearby village of Knock, and has parts dating from the 12th century together with a range of splendidly grotesque gargoyles. When the lead-mining 'boom' arrived in the 18th century, the old settlement was considerably expanded and redeveloped by the London Lead Company. The prominent annular fountain with lion's head on the village green is a company donation, but is constructed from the local sandstone rather than following the pattern-book wrought-iron designs found at the other company villages of Middleton and Nenthead. When mining ended, Dufton relaxed back into the cosy insularity of the other East Fellside villages, but its popularity then increased significantly again as the village became established as an important staging post on the route of the Pennine Way.

Scordale

The Pennine Way reaches Dufton from Upper Teesdale by one of the most spectacular sights in the North Pennines: *High Cup Nick*. On the approach over the wild moors from Birkdale by Maize Beck, the actual watershed is crossed to the threshold of the Eden valley in a surprisingly short distance. A flat plain adorned with limestone outcrops leads to the point where the ground suddenly falls away in an abrupt chasm to reveal the High Cup valley far below. In his 1898 book on Upper Teesdale, James Backhouse provides a shepherd lad's description of this famous route over the Pennines, which encapsulates the journey into a few appropriately succinct words:

'Well, gang ower t'moor and ye'll come ti a greeart goolf, an it opens out inter toother country'

The point of arrival at the 'greeart goolf' marks the apex of a converging horseshoe of crags that encircles the valley head. This dramatic place is traditionally referred to as High Cup Nick, although rather intriguingly some old maps label it as Eagle's Chair suggesting an eyrie probably existed here in times past. Today, ravens can occasionally be seen amongst the crags, diving and darting acrobatically on the local air currents, this site being one of their traditional haunts despite a recent decline.

The long symmetrical escarpments of dark dolerite at the rim of the valley are a result of the Whin Sill outcropping on either side of the valley. The whinstone rocks have then been eroded and weathered into columnar pillars, often producing a pleated effect in the play of light and shade. In places, further weathering has produced pinnacle features, such as the notable obelisk of Nichol's Last on the northern crags; this is said to be named from the local cobbler who climbed it and then repaired a pair of boots on its tiny summit! Below the cliffs, large angular blocks of scree mantle the steep slopes descending to the flat valley floor. Down there amongst the green turf of the valley bottom, a vigorous stream bubbles out of springs below the boulders and then steadily winds its way down towards the distant Eden valley.

> *... the path led directly to High Cup Gill and a different world. It was as though we had gone through a door, exchanging a dull room for one filled with sunshine. It was a scene filled with wonder and it spilled into our lives and enriched them.*
>
> *Discovering the Eden valley*, Charlie Emmet 2005

A corner of Dufton village with Dufton Pike behind

The 'greeart goolf': High Cup Nick

High Cup: note the almost-vertical dry-stone wall up the slope on the far right

The great rift-valley itself is named High Cup, a most appropriate name from an Eden valley perspective as it a forms a deep amphitheatre in the Pennine escarpment between Murton Fell and Backstone Edge. The Nick is actually a cleft in the cliffs, elevated in status because of its location on the path at the great moment of arrival across the watershed. The distinctive U-shaped profile of High Cup is unique compared to the normal V-shape of the other East Fellside 'dales'. Clearly it has been etched by ice, and presumably this flowed from a local ice-cap that accumulated on the high fells in the same manner that valley glaciers in the High Arctic or Norway are currently nourished by plateau ice-caps. The presence of the Whin Sill outcropping at the valley rim has been the key factor in producing the symmetrical concave profile of the valley sides, with the scree slopes masking the less resistant rocks below. The breach in the cliffs at the head of the valley would have been the route for a torrent of meltwater pouring off the fells as the glacier ice melted.

On either side of High Cup, streams cascade down the upper slopes and over the precipitous rocks of the escarpment, the water often being lashed back upwards in sharp gusts of wind. As a band of limestone exists above the whinstone, lime is washed down over the crags encouraging hanging gardens of plants and ferns. On the north side, at the rocky ledges of Narrow Gate, the path exhilaratingly crosses one of these cascading streams below where it gushes to the surface at the crystal-clear spring of Hannah's Well. Overlooking the scene are the prominent cairns on the crest at Narrowgate Beacon behind which the featureless plateau is redeemed by containing three large tarns; in general, the North Pennines have few natural lakes, although there are many that have been artificially created by dams across streams. Another conspicuous feature at High Cup is the remarkable wall that was, in times past and for reasons unknown, built straight up the steep slopes on the south side. The craftsmanship of the wall is evident by the fact that even now, despite the predations of climate and terrain, much of it remains intact.

The next three side-valleys, Great Rundale, Swindale and Knock Ore Gill, have the normal V-shape profile of East Fellside valleys. They also bear clear signs of mining activity, particularly in the 'hushes' channelled into the fellside. As with Scordale, after lead mining ceased at the end of the 19th century, barytes became the main mineral extracted, initially from within the mine and then until quite recently by foraging amongst the old spoil heaps. *Milburn* is the main settlement on this section of the East Fellside, with the houses delightfully arranged around a wide green and maypole, accessed by a narrow entrance at each corner. Nearby is Howgill Castle, a modified 14th century pele house of massive proportions with walls over 3m thick.

The northern escarpment: High Cup

Milburn

Great Rundale

Dunfell Hush

From the sprawling slopes of Knock Fell, the main Pennine range continues over Great Dun Fell, with its prominent radar station, to Little Dun Fell and then the massive bulk of Cross Fell. The long-distance path of the Pennine Way traverses these four summits before descending to Garrigill in South Tynedale. The massif provides the largest area of high ground over 700m in England, with the culminating summit, Cross Fell, having a particular reputation for surliness. Conditions on Cross Fell are usually a 'world' away from those down in the valley and, in such circumstances, the original name of Fiends' Fell seems rather more apposite. According to legend, the fell was renamed when St. Paulinus, the first Bishop of York, erected a cross to banish the evil spirits; some versions of the tale, however, nominate St. Augustine or St. Ninian as the exorcist. Nevertheless, the fiends do not appear to have retreated very far, the name now applying to another fell near to Hartside Cross.

Traces of mining extend onto the highest slopes of these fells in particularly remote situations, much of it the work of the 'Old Man'. The spectacular ravine of Dunfell Hush below the radar station indicates repeated use of the scouring effect of water to expose and exploit a lead vein. German miners possibly worked here in Elizabethan times: they were certainly active at that time on Alston Moor and some of the names at the Dunfell mines imply a link, such as Henrake Hush being 'Heinrich's hush'. Miners also discovered natural subterranean passages at Knock Fell Caverns and Silverband Caverns, formed from water dissolving through a band of limestone that girdles the fell. Tracks up Knock Ore Gill and Trout Beck (Teesdale) would have provided access for the miners, and the drovers sometimes used this way ('Knockergill Pass') from South Tynedale to the Eden valley. At a later stage, the London Lead Company built a road along this route, the Trout Beck section now having been eroded away whilst the Knock Ore Gill track has become the access road for the radar station. The mine at Silverband was worked for barytes until very recently, with the rusty pylons indicating the remains of an aerial ropeway.

All approaches to Cross Fell involve a final climb through the necklace of large gritstone boulders that form an 'edge' to the flat summit plateau. Typically, the exposed position of the summit will mean that it is cold and windy on arrival. The low temperatures on the plateau have favoured the development of tundra (periglacial) features produced by the heaving and sorting action of ice crystals, including earth hummocks, stone polygons and stone stripes. Remarkably in a bygone age of hardier people, political rallies and sports events used to take place here; in 1832, fifty brass bands are said to have massed to celebrate the historic passing of the Reform Bill. There is also a long tradition of climbing to the summit to view the sunrise in mid-summer.

'God's Golf Ball'

A conspicuous feature from many viewpoints both in the Eden valley and Teesdale (also from higher parts of South Tynedale), especially in the glinting sun, is the large white radar dome on Great Dun Fell. Local people irreverently refer to this unmistakeable landmark as 'God's Golf Ball'. A meteorological station was first established here in 1948, following on from Gordon Manley's investigation of the Helm Wind (p.40), and the fell subsequently sprouted a series of communication masts. In 1985, the Civil Aviation Authority built the radar dome with monitoring station, and this acts as one of the key navigation waymarks for aircraft in UK airspace.

With the passage of time, negative perceptions of the distracting appearance of the dome have perhaps softened a little, although its contrast with the Pennine landscape remains starkly alien. On the positive side, the access road can provide rapid access to the high fells, a benefit sometimes used by skiers in search of good snow. Also, the station weather data are now generally available online in real-time mode, so that up-to-the-hour conditions on the high tops can be obtained directly rather than inferred from other sources.

The summit of Cross Fell, looking south

Great Dun Fell with 'golf ball' from Knock Fell

Cross Fell from Melmerby Fell, to the north

The Helm Wind

*There's Cross Fell too, with cloud-capt head,
Bepatch'd with winter's snow;
From whose dark helm the hurricanes
Descend and houl below;*

Isaac Ritson
from *'A history of Cumberland'*
William Hutchison 1794

Cross Fell with typical cloud cap

If a brisk wind is blowing on the East Fellside, then it should be hoped that it is not coming from the north-east quadrant. This is the direction that characterises the notorious Helm Wind when it tempestuously shrieks down from the Pennine tops. At such times, crops are desiccated, soils scoured, roofs dislodged and barns dismantled. Its force and duration can terrify farm animals and fray the nerves of humans. Walking and breathing become difficult and the constant roaring induces headaches and tetchiness. Local folklore even describes how it can blow the tails off cows or the 'nebs' off geese!

When the Helm is 'on', the main effects are experienced in a wide swathe west of the Pennines extending from Warcop to Renwick, and the severity of the wind is distinctive in not extending west beyond the River Eden. A large threatening mass of cloud ('The Helm') sits on Cross Fell and its satellites during this time, often accompanied by a sliver of open sky and sunlight over the lower slopes. Another cloud ('The Bar') typically demarcates the western limit of this open sky at a distance some 5-10km from the fells; this secondary cloud is a more ephemeral feature, but when it does form it has a tendency to exhibit a distinct whirling or rotating motion.

The extreme behaviour of the Helm Wind can be attributed to the topography of the North Pennines and the location of the East Fellside. Although William Marriott from the Royal Meteorological Society had made insightful suggestions in the late 19th century, the first detailed explanation was provided by Professor Gordon Manley of Durham University in the 1940s. In the best tradition of scientific interpretation based upon empirical observation, Manley spent a considerable amount of time on Great Dun Fell gathering data. His main shelter was a small rudimentary hut, transported there by a local farmer. Despite the capricious nature of the Wind, which meant that it was typically not blowing when Manley was present, his field data supported a theory that he had been testing. The key feature of this explanation is the ramp-like cross-section of the North Pennines, with a gently rising east flank and a sharp fall westwards into the Eden valley. The western escarpment is also straight and regular because of its fault-line origin, and its steep slopes are now generally quite smooth because they have been mainly denuded of trees.

Two main climatic conditions are required for the Helm to blow. Firstly, the wind needs to be blowing from the north-east quadrant, and at a brisk speed, typically more than Beaufort Force 3 on the east coast, equating with a minimum of Force 5 (35km/h) on the top of Great Dun Fell. Secondly, a temperature inversion needs to be present in the lower atmosphere, such that above a height of about 1800m, the air is warmer and acts as a capping layer by trapping the cold air beneath. The result of these conditions is that, as air is blown up across the Pennines from the north-east, it is forced to rise, whilst also being squeezed and funnelled by the capping inversion into a narrower space. On reaching the abrupt western escarpment, the confinement is released allowing a jet of cold air to blast down the steep slope into the Eden valley. The wind frequently reaches Force 9 on the upper slopes, falling to Force 7-8 below, and at these speeds inevitably causes some devastation.

When the descending air meets the valley floor it often produces a 'rebound' effect. In technical terms, this is the characteristic fluid behaviour (a 'hydraulic jump') found in standing wave effects, as in a river falling over a weir. The 'rebound' causes the air to abruptly rise again, and as it does so, it cools and the water vapour condenses to cloud. This produces the distinctive cloud feature of 'The Bar', contrasting with the typically open skies produced by the descending air before it rebounds upwards. The whirling motion of 'The Bar' is a product of the turbulent eddies produced when the ascending air dissipates through friction. As it does so, the energy of the wind jet rapidly declines, meaning its effects do not travel much further west. On the ground, observers below 'The Bar' will note that the wind is almost calm, and to the west beyond the 'rebound' effect it may become brisk again, but its force is very much reduced from the actual Helm Wind itself.

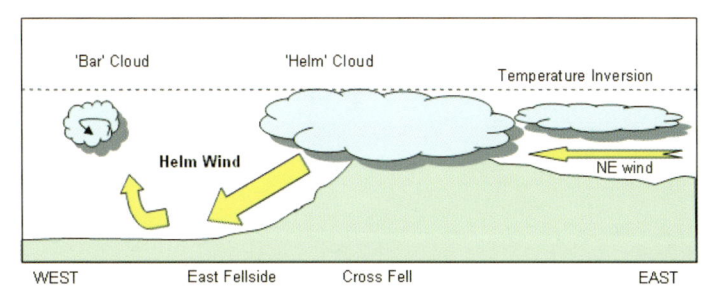

There are many other eccentricities of the Helm Wind which seasoned local observers have characterised. For instance, there is a 'Black Helm' and a 'White Helm' depending on the colour of the cloud cap. Also possible are 'Two-barred Helms' and in extreme conditions, even a 'Five-barred Helm', depending on the number of 'Bar' clouds visible, and presumably the dynamics of the rebound effect. Sometimes, when no 'Bar' is present, the wind blasts down to the valley without any significant rebound at all. It can also be observed that the irregular hills of the Pikes, which are one of the few discontinuities along the escarpment, can sometimes produce their own clouds, rather like rocks causing eddies in a stream.

Although similar phenomena ('lee waves') occur in other mountain ranges (with turbulent 'rotor' effects known to pilots), nowhere else in this country do they have a distinctive name, nor such a fearsome reputation or folklore. The slope of the Pennine escarpment above the East Fellside seems to be at just the appropriate angle for the wind jet to flow down it without separating from the ground surface and producing a sheltering effect as would occur behind steep cliffs. The prevailing meteorological conditions for the wind are most common in spring and autumn, but it can occur at any time of year. Another notable observation is that it generally disappears at night (it is then said to have 'gone to bed'), presumably because the temperature inversion over the fell tops lowers at this time as the cold air sinks to the valleys, preventing the wind jet from developing.

As may be expected, long experience of the Helm Wind means that the Fellside villages have adapted to its effects. Typically buildings are arranged with their backs to the most vulnerable wind direction, with doors and windows on the lee-side and streets at right angles to avoid funnelling effects. The most exposed villages are considered to be Milburn, Kirkland, Ousby, Melmerby and Gamblesby, probably because they are closest to the steep slopes down which the wind blows.

Kirkland church

The East Fellside villages continue northwards with Blencarn, Kirkland, Skirwith and Ousby, each featuring a distinctive church built from the warm local stone. By contrast, the grandly-named Hanging Gardens of Mark Anthony tend to disappoint, being remnants of old cultivation terraces surpassed by better if less romantically-named examples elsewhere. From Kirkland, the 'Maiden Way' created by the Romans climbs onto the fells past the currick of Man at Edge. Its slanting course provides a reasonably well-graded route up the steep fellside and the track was later adopted into a regular drovers' way. The flanking valley to the south of the Roman road is the deep recess of Ardale, at the head of which is the dripping whinstone crag of Black Doors and a series of small local coal pits.

Melmerby is another charming village sitting at the base of the fells, where the only road to breach this section of the Pennines begins its long climb to Hartside Cross. As with nearby Ousby (from Ulfsby, or Ulf's settlement), the name of Melmerby (Melmer's settlement) harks back to the early Scandanavian settlers who cleared and occupied these marginal locations. The fellside here is characterised by rather unnatural rectilinear-shaped plantations, which may provide some limited local protection against the Helm Wind. Trials were made for lead in this vicinity but the veins were not very productive, therefore farming and catering for wayfarers have remained the dominant village activities.

The serpentine ascent from Melmerby to *Hartside Cross* provides one of the longest road climbs in the country, in addition to it having one of the highest summits at 575m. The old route up to the pass was rather different from the present road, climbing more directly up the slopes from Gamblesby, then over Twotop Hill. This was one of the routes that was considerably improved upon by John McAdam, whilst working for the London Lead Company. The many twists and turns of the road are necessary adjustments not only to the harsh gradient but also to cross several dry channels etched in the hillside, relics of the extensive suite of glacial meltwater routes found at many different levels on the flanks of the Eden valley.

The road summit and café at Hartside Cross is inevitably a popular halt for travellers, providing a superb panorama on a clear day, as eulogised by Thomas Sopwith (p.115) in his classic 1833 book and more obliquely by WH Auden. On particularly propitious occasions, a sea of cloud obscures the valley below, whilst the fells are cloud-free, further enhancing the prospect across to the serrated skyline of Lakeland. In less favourable circumstances, snow and ice can make the road treacherous: not surprisingly, this is one of the first Pennine routes to be closed in adverse conditions.

The Lakeland skyline from Hartside Cross

On the lowland plain nearby is the Neolithic site of *Long Meg and her Daughters*, one of the largest stone circles in Britain. Long Meg stands apart from the other stones in the group, inscribed with enigmatic circles and spirals that were probably added later during the Bronze Age (2000-900 BC). From the centre of the circle, the winter sun sets behind Long Meg at the solstice, indicating its role as a primeval calendar. The name of the site is said to come from the legend of a coven of witches turned into stone at this location by a magician.

Long Meg and her Daughters

The villages just to the north of the Hartside road are amongst the most attractive in the Eden valley, each with their neat churches. At the foot of the fells are Gamblesby and Renwick, whilst closer to the River Eden and less exposed to the Helm Wind are Glassonby and Kirkoswald. The cluster of buildings around the cobbled square at *Kirkoswald* are particularly distinctive and charming; the parish church of St. Oswald's stands a short distance away behind a distinctive conical hillock, on the summit of which is a detached bell tower. Below the west wall of the church is an ancient well, served by a small metal cup on a chain, which is reputed to have led to the original founding of an ecclesiastical building here by St. Aidan in the 7th century. The old castle nearby is now only a gaunt shell but in its heyday could boast one of the finest great halls in northern England: it dates back to about 1200AD and was gradually modified and strengthened thereafter whilst being encircled by a large moat. The remains of another significant fortified building can be found at Haresceugh, where there was formerly a large tower-house.

Although the Pennine escarpment continues in the same abrupt form, the fells north of Hartside become more shapeless, extending as an extensive swathe of tussock grass and bog from Black Fell to Cold Fell. They are rarely trodden, except occasionally by farmers rounding-up errant sheep or itinerant fellwalkers. Miners have worked the slopes of the escarpment for lead and barytes in the past but no large-scale developments resulted from their efforts. In the midst of this vast tract of featureless country is the curio of Tom Smith's Stone, a boundary marker on the Northumberland-Cumbria border inscribed with the letters A C K W on each side (Alston, Croglin, Knarsdale and Whitley).

Looking northwards from near Hartside Cross towards Thack Moor

The Eden Gorge and William Mounsey

Between Kirkoswald and Wetheral, the Eden has carved a magnificent gorge through the soft sandstone. This provides the setting for a beautiful mix of natural woodlands and newer plantations that occupy the valley and often overhang the precipitous red rocks of the gorge. In their midst, the rejuvenated river flows swiftly through a series of sweeping curves broken by occasional rapids. In addition to its status as a famous salmon run, the river also contains other notable aquatic species, including lampreys, bullheads, and crayfish.

The Eden is essentially unregulated throughout its course, receiving many large tributaries from the Pennines and eastern Lakeland, and therefore being prone to severe flooding. At such times, the adjacent land is swamped by a swirling mass of chocolate-coloured water complete with a mix of entrained flotsam and jetsam swept into its flow. Some of these large floods have entered into local folklore. For example, the infamous flood of winter 1822 devastated much of the valley, including Appleby, where the parish church was inundated with over a metre of water. More recently, in January 2005, severe flooding caused extensive damage and loss of livestock throughout the valley.

There are several locations in the gorge worthy of note, although access is not straightforward because of occasional forestry activities and a sometimes rather over-zealous protection of fishing and shooting rights. At the Chain Rock, near Lazonby, 30m high rocks hang directly over the river. On the opposite bank are the famous Nunnery Walks, where the Croglin Water joins the Eden in a tumult of foaming water; the walks are privately-owned and named from the Benedictine nunnery established at nearby Staffield.

Perhaps the most varied section of the river is at Armathwaite. Upstream from the village is a spectacular cataract where the river leaps over an abrupt discontinuity in its bed (photo p.47). Often, salmon can be seen attempting to jump this fall, leaping intuitively against the force of the water. The regular structure of the barrier feature may suggest an artificial weir, but in fact the smooth dark rock is a natural formation known to geologists as the Armathwaite Dyke and which represents a narrow intrusion of magma into the surrounding sandstones. The resulting basalt-like rock (tholeiite) has resisted erosion and therefore forms a barrier (a dyke) to the smooth flow of the river.

A little further upstream from the Armathwaite Dyke, a series of sandstone cliffs rises directly out of the river. If the water level is not too high, it is possible to follow the riverbank to view the enigmatic carvings made on these rocks by William Mounsey in the 19th century. These consist of a series of rotund faces accompanied by a written inscription (some letters are reversed) parodying Isaac Walton's verses in 'The Compleat Angler':

The Fisher's gentle life,
Happiest is of any;
Void of pleasure, full of strife,
And beloved by many;
Others are but toys,
And to be lamented,
Only this a pleasure is.

Mounsey came from the old smugglers' village of Rockcliffe on the Solway marshes, and had unusually extensive and diverse interests for his time. In particular, he developed an almost spiritual link with the Eden. During 1850, he followed the river to its source and erected a stone there with Greek and Latin inscriptions: unfortunately it was later destroyed by railway workers who were apparently disturbed by the strange languages and symbols. His handiwork can also be seen by the river at the rock chambers of Constantine Cells in Wetheral woods, where monks from the nearby priory hid their valuables from border raiders. In addition to his verse on the 'Ituna' (Eden) found at the head of this chapter he has inscribed the following lines on the rock, which are taken from the Welsh bard Llywarch Wen:

The leaf which is being persecuted by the wind,
let her beware of her fate.
She is old though only born this year

The River Eden near Armathwaite; William Mounsey's face carvings are inscribed on the rocks to the left

A little further north, the pleasant village of *Croglin* (formerly Crokelyn) is most notable for the conspicuous church of St. John the Baptist. The vicarage opposite the church was originally a pele tower next to the manor house, but later the buildings were adapted into a comfortable Georgian house. In the nearby vicinity are traces of a Bronze Age settlement and the intriguing hamlet of Scarrowmanwick located in a key defensive position on a high ridge above the valley.

The village of Croglin is most well-known outside of the district for its macabre vampire story of 1875, as reported by the august body of the 'Gentleman's Magazine' at the time. Amelia Cranswell, one of the tenants of Croglin Low Hall, was said to have been bitten on her neck during the night by a dark bat-like figure clad in a grave-shroud. When a doctor examined her, he concluded that the injuries were most likely to have been caused by an animal rather than a human. The shocked Cranswell family then took the victim away from the Hall on holiday to allow her to recuperate, but when they returned, the figure again appeared to her at night. Alerted by the victim's cries, the shadowy menace was confronted and shot at by the other tenants of the hall, then pursued to the church crypt. Next morning, when the hastily-assembled local militia entered the crypt, they discovered a shrouded body with bloody fangs. To end the torment, they attacked the body in traditional manner, dispatching it with a rowan-wood stake through the heart.

Curiously, the village of Renwick, to the south also has a vampire legend. The creature is said to have been disturbed when the old church there was demolished in 1845. The bat-like figure then proceeded to terrorise the local people until it was again hunted down and finished off with a rowan-wood stake. As with most legends, there is an initial sound basis for these stories which appear to have become embellished over time, so that they then contain supposition and inconsistencies.

The last remaining villages along the northern section of fellside, before the Geltsdale section is reached, are Newbiggin and Cumrew. Both villages are small linear groups of buildings, located just off the main valley road, overlooked by attractive woodlands that continue to flourish on the steep hillside. On a small hill above the woods are the remains of an old castle that once commanded a strategic outlook over both villages and the valley approaches. The fellside above the two villages rises to Cardunneth Pike, marked by the large prominent cairn on its crest that is of some antiquity. Excavations conducted at the site of the cairn in the 19th century revealed the bones of a human skeleton indicating that these western slopes of the North Pennines still have many mysteries yet to reveal.

Croglin Church

Glassonby

St. Lawrence's Church, Appleby

Armathwaite Dyke

Dufton Pike

Murton

Barnard Castle

Lower Teesdale and Greta

Where Tees, full many a fathom low,
Wears his rage no common foe
Rokeby, Sir Walter Scott

The lower section of Teesdale provides a broader, more pastoral landscape than the upper part of the valley. Villages become more common, and the bounding fells are of lesser height, generally forming a wide expanse of moor extending from the desolation of Stainmore in the west. This area of the North Pennines is well-known for its attractive villages and beautiful river scenery, a quality further enhanced by the rich historical associations. In addition, a series of tributary streams and rivers flow vigorously off the western moors, each with their distinctive character: most notable of these is the Greta, which has established its own literary renown.

The focal point for this lovely district is the market town of *Barnard Castle* (or *'Barney'* to the familiar). The castle itself dominates the western approaches to the town, guarding the strategic bridge crossing over the Tees. Its gaunt appearance and imposing position on a crag above the river provide a dramatic scene, and one that inspired paintings by both JMW Turner and John Sell Cotman. The graceful arches spanning the river are still traditionally referred to as the County Bridge: until 1974 the river formed the county boundary between Durham and Yorkshire along much of its length. Earlier, the Romans had forded the river a little upstream when building their road between Bowes and Binchester, a crossing point still remembered in the place-name of Startforth ('street ford') on the west bank.

The early castle was founded by Guy de Baliol in the 11th century and named after his nephew Bernard who substantially expanded it. However, when a successor, John Baliol, made and lost his claim for the vacant Scottish crown in the 14th century, it became forfeit and granted to the Warwick/Neville dynasty, before passing back to the crown (Richard III) through marriage. Surprisingly, compared to other castles in the area, it has not seen a great deal of military action, perhaps because of its daunting appearance. Its most notable event was in 1569 during the 'Rising of the North', when the castle endured an eleven-day siege by a force of about 5000 Catholic rebels supporting Mary Queen of Scots against Elizabeth I. The sympathies of the townsfolk were generally with the attackers rather than the defenders, and when the outer castle ward fell, cutting off the water supply, surrender became inevitable. In the meantime, thirty-five of the defenders were killed or maimed jumping from the walls. Nevertheless, while the siege continued, it allowed time for opposing forces to mass elsewhere, and although the castle did yield, the rebellion was soon quashed.

JMW Turner and John Sell Cotman

The artist JMW Turner came to Teesdale through meeting JBS Morritt, owner of Rokeby Hall and wealthy patron of the arts. During his many visits to the area, as encouraged by Morritt, he would stay at Rokeby in order to explore the local landscape and paint some of its scenery and landmarks. Amongst his extensive repertoire of paintings are impressive representations of natural scenes such as the Meeting of the Waters, High Force and Cauldron Snout, but he also painted the dramatic buildings of Egglestone Abbey and Barnard Castle.

John Sell Cotman is a less well-known painter, but his landscape watercolours are widely lauded now for their aesthetic quality, contrasting with Turner's sense of drama and movement. JBS Moritt engaged Cotman in 1805 to provide painting lessons for his wife, and the artist used the opportunity to paint several local scenes. Probably the most notable of these is his refined study of Greta Bridge which was captured on canvas in 1807, the painting now being housed in the British Museum.

Under the patronage of the castle, a prosperous market town developed and grew. The market cross is the unusual two-tiered building of the Buttermarket sitting at the top of The Bank, which as well being the hub of the market, was also formerly the site of a small town hall and jail. A suite of fine 18th and 19th century buildings characterises the old town, with Blargroves House on The Bank dating from the late

16th century. However, the most striking building in the town is situated along Newgate, where the lavish French chateau of *Bowes Museum* amply earns its admiring but irreverent moniker as 'The Taj Mahal of the North'. The building was begun as a project in 1860 by John Bowes, Earl of Strathmore and wealthy coal baron, together with his French wife. It thereafter became a repository for their extensive art collection, and nowadays has developed into an excellent museum featuring local history exhibits as well as hosting the renowned art galleries.

One part of Barnard Castle that has changed significantly is the riverside district of Bridgegate and Thorngate. Based on the abundant local supply, this was the centre of the town's woollen industry, being particularly known for its stockings and 'tammies' (bonnets). The big flood of 1771 inundated some of the properties, and at one of them the floodwaters dyed the tammies a very unusual colour that proved very popular in London, but could not be reproduced again! In the 19th century, mills producing woven-wool carpets took over the riverside with the workers housed nearby in densely-grouped tenements. Overcrowding and poor sanitary conditions were prime circumstances for the spread of disease, including a severe outbreak of cholera in 1849. The large Ullathorne's Mill on the west bank was demolished in 1976 and Thorngate Mill is now converted to residential flats. The substantial Thorngate footbridge was built in 1882 to replace an ill-conceived previous structure that lasted only ten years before being swept away by floods. Downstream are the popular open spaces of the Demesnes, an area originally granted to local people by the castle overlord and traditionally used for the drilling of militia.

Seven kilometres south-west along the Roman road from Barnard Castle is the large village of *Bowes*, owing its prominence to the key position on the historic road over Stainmore. The relationship between traveller and village is testified by its long straggling rows of houses along the old road (the village now being bypassed by the A66). Being situated at the edge of the inhospitable moors, this was one of the historic staging posts where travellers could halt and relieve the rigours of the journey. In earlier times, the Romans had built a large fort (*Lavatrae*) at this location which was notable for containing a bathhouse apparently supplied by an aqueduct built from Deepdale across the moor to the north. The massive castle keep overlooking the village dates from Norman times, with the thickness of its walls and robust compact design demonstrating the structural strength considered necessary to repel regular raids by the Scots. Despite this, the castle was abandoned in the 14th century after being repeatedly damaged by raiders and squabbled over by kings, archbishops and barons.

Charles Dickens and the 'Yorkshire Schools'

Mrs. Squeers stood at one end of the desks, presiding over an immense basin of brimstone and treacle, of which delicious compound she administered a large instalment to each boy in succession ......they all being obliged, under heavy corporal penalties, to take in the whole of the bowl at a gasp.
Nicholas Nickleby, Charles Dickens

At the west end of Bowes village is the large building once known as Shaw's Academy, one of the notorious 'Yorkshire Schools', and now as Dotheboys Hall. There were three other such schools in the village and about twenty in the wider vicinity. It was Shaw's Academy, however, that became the model for the grim establishment portrayed by Charles Dickens in 'Nicholas Nickleby'. To collect material for the book, Dickens visited the area in 1838, posing as a prospective parent. His sense of social justice had earlier been alerted by the poor reputation of the schools. Widely-disseminated advertisements explicitly referred to the lack of school vacations, implying that it was an ideal repository for unwanted boys with minimum inconvenience to parents or guardians.

Although Dickens undoubtedly used artistic licence, and some of the evidence is hearsay, conditions in the schools were undoubtedly severe. In 1823, fifteen years before Dickens wrote his book, Shaw had been sued by the parents of two children who had become blind through infection and neglect. The trial heard how the boys were beaten and supplied with maggot-ridden food, with up to five boys sharing the same flea-infested bed. Shaw was convicted and as a consequence had to pay £300 in damages, but was still allowed to run his school. It is also known that boarders were sent to work on nearby farms to earn extra money for their masters. Most tellingly, local churchyards have the graves of several children from the schools: Bowes church has gravestones for twenty-five pupils. However, the negative publicity garnered by 'Nicholas Nickleby' soon turned the business into a sharp decline.

Below the village, the River Greta darts through the woodlands in a sweeping bend from which Bowes may have originally obtained its name (from the Norse 'bogr' meaning 'bow'). The river's name is apparently derived from the Norse 'griótá' meaning 'rocky stream', an appropriate description for its rock-carved or stony channel. Next to the site of the old Bowes mill, the river forms the charming beauty spot of Mill Force where it cascades over a rock shelf into a wide pool. An unusual prehistoric hoard of 123 bronze axes has been found near here. Upstream of the village, green pastures and the lively flow of the Greta alleviate the bleak moors traversed by the Stainmore highway. At *God's Bridge* there is a remarkable natural rock bridge where a block of limestone spans the river channel at the point where it enters an interesting gorge. A series of subterranean passages exist here, with the bridge apparently the last remnant of a cavern through which the river flowed before its roof collapsed. Normally the river-bed is dry at this point, except for a pool under the bridge itself where the cave passage re-emerges. However, after heavy rain, when the becks are 'brimmin', the underground passages become flooded and the previously dry surface channel surges with foaming peaty water.

Bowes Castle

Mill Force

God's Bridge

The Trough

Greta Bridge

An old drove road crosses the fells to reach the Greta valley at God's Bridge. This same route is now followed by the Pennine Way, which, travelling northward, reaches God's Bridge by pleasant walking from the isolated farmstead at Sleightholme. The path across the fields allows a few peeks into the impressive depths of The Trough, where a tributary stream of the Greta enters its own interesting limestone gorge. South of Sleightholme, the Pennine Way has a less savoury reputation, traversing a rough section of moor from Tan Hill. In his inimitable 'Pennine Way Companion' guidebook, Alfred Wainwright likened this passage to walking through porridge, although he also indicated that after heavy rain it further deteriorated to the consistency of oxtail soup!

The vast swathe of Bowes Moor can at times seem monotonous and drab, but in late summer it comes ablaze as the heather blooms. There are few prominent landmarks on the moor, one of them being provided by the irregular knolls of the Seven Hills near to Sleightholme, formed from debris dumped by the last glaciers. Another interesting feature occurs at Huggill Force, where the stream provides a pleasant waterfall as it leaps the final section to the river valley in a lacy cascade.

North of Bowes, the featureless moors extending towards Deepdale are given a rather eerie aura by the remains of old military buildings and sinister warning notices. This was a testing area for mustard gas, now abandoned and seemingly forgotten. Even here though there are surprises, particularly at the isolated farmstead of Levy Pool. As with many other upland farms, this row of buildings was abandoned and left to slowly moulder into overgrown ruins, a particularly sad fate because the dwelling dated back to 1776 and an outbuilding had one of the few remaining 'black thack' heather-thatched roofs in the country. However, now an encouraging restoration is underway and Levy Pool once again bears signs of life and hope.

The lower course of the Greta is one of the hidden gems of the North Pennines. After a quieter interlude, the river passes under Rutherford Bridge (on the The Stang road to Arkengarthdale) to enter a deep wooded gorge. From here down to Greta Bridge it sparkles its way through a series of sun-dappled glades and leafy bowers amidst secretive overgrown cliffs. A myriad woodland flowers spangle the slopes in spring and summer, whilst in autumn the paths become a golden tapestry of fallen leaves. These are the famous *Brignall Banks*, immortalised by Walter Scott, and certainly still 'wild and fair' for all.

Deep within the recesses of the Greta valley in a clearing by the river is the site of the old St. Mary's Church of Brignall, another of the scenes painted by Turner. The remains of the 13th century structure stand in a walled enclosure together with a hoary array of gravestones and tombs. In 1833, the parish church was moved up the hill to its present site with the other village buildings of Brignall, using some of the stone from the old church. Between the old church and Brignall Mill, also delightfully located in a woodland clearing, the river runs through a rough, craggy gorge with accompanying paths. A rudimentary stone shelter in the rocks of the gorge marks the meditative retreat of an aesthete who particularly appreciated this wild scene. On the south side of the valley is the hamlet of Scargill with the crumbling ruins of its old castle, and the lovely village of Barningham arranged around a broad green backed by swelling moors.

Sir Walter Scott and 'Rokeby'

*O, Brignall banks are wild and fair,
And Greta woods are green,
And you may gather garlands there,
Would grace a summer queen*

JBS Morritt of Rokeby Hall was also the link between Sir Walter Scott and Teesdale. After meeting Scott in both Edinburgh and London, Morritt invited him and his wife to visit Rokeby, which they first did in 1809. During this and subsequent visits, Scott became inspired by the local scenery and set about melding a germ of an idea about a poem set during the Civil War with the surrounding landscape. Much of this contextualising took place in the grounds of Rokeby Park, with the author ensconced by the river in a rough cave complete with seat and table.

The resulting epic poem was 'Rokeby', a romantic picture of chivalry and grandeur in Scott's archetypal style. Some may quibble with the end product: critics have dismissed the rhythmic style upon which the poem relies as a series of 'lumbering quartos'. Nevertheless, there are some fine resonant lines in its verses, notably the opening scene when a warden on the walls of Barnard Castle scans the land for news of battle, and of course the celebrated lines sung by a minstrel describing the delights of Brignall Banks.

Greta Bridge marks the historic river crossing and long-time travellers' halt on the Roman road over Stainmore. Formerly, there were three inns here to cater for the needs of wayfarers: now only one remains, and in the fields behind the Morritt Arms can be seen traces of the Roman fort established at this site. The graceful arched bridge, fortunately now bypassed by the A66 highway, was built in 1789 to a design by John Carr of York, replacing an earlier structure: it later provided the subject for John Sell Cotman's most well-known painting. Just upstream of the bridge, the river squeezes through the rocky constrictions and rapids of Hell's Cauldron.

The old church of St. Mary's at Brignall

Brignall Mill

THE NORTH PENNINES

Greta Bridge also marks one of the entrances to Rokeby Park, through which the River Greta flows in its last section. The Palladian-style mansion hall forming the centrepiece of the park was built for Sir Thomas Robinson in 1720: it then passed to the Morritt family, of whom JBS Morritt became a key figure in the cultural and artistic development of the district. The river dashes through the park in a rocky channel overhung by dark foliage, passing Scott's cave, to finally debouch into the Tees at the famous *Meeting of the Water*s. The final channel of the Greta is a succession of fissures and deep pools, strewn with boulders and other debris before finally being swept away by the dark waters of the parent river. Overlooking the scene is the rustic span of Dairy Bridge, almost engulfed by ivy; a small Gothic-style house sits at one end of the bridge with a balcony overlooking the surging waters. Legend says that under the bridge was once confined a headless ghost, a lady of the Rokeby family murdered by raiders, but the restless spirit is now reputed to have escaped and is free to haunt the whole of the park at night.

On the hill above Dairy Bridge is the conspicious landmark of Mortham Tower. This was the medieval seat of the Rokeby family which had begun as a 14th century pele house and was then extended into a 15th century courtyard manor house with arched gateway. The fortifications and walled enclosure for stockading cattle would have provided considerable protection against the marauding brigands of that time. In Turner's painting of the 'Meeting of the Waters' as seen from the north bank of the Tees, the tower house is illuminated on its hill by the pale light of a crescent moon.

The River Greta in Rokeby Park

The Meeting of the Waters

The Tees at the 'Paradise Walk', near Rokeby

Abbey Bridge

Riverside rocks at Whorlton

The 'Rock Walk' upriver of Barnard Castle

The Tees below Barnard Castle is an effervescent accompaniment to the splendid riverside paths that run along either bank. At Abbey Gorge, the waters rush into a narrow rocky channel bordered by solid waterworn slabs of limestone, the same rock which was locally quarried as 'Teesdale marble'. The gorge is spanned by the crenulated battlements and lofty arch of Abbey Bridge, formerly a toll-crossing, and built by the Morritts of Rokeby. These features are named from *Egglestone Abbey* which stands as an impressive ruin on the south bank (photo: p.16). The abbey was founded in the 12th century by the White Canons of the Premontratensian order, occupying a typically secluded valley location. Fortunately, enough remains of the transepts and nave of the Abbey church, together with the outline of the surrounding buildings, to give an impression of its character and scale, although it was generally one of the poorer monasteries. Just below the abbey, next to the road, can be seen the arch of Bow Bridge, a quaint 17th Century packhorse structure.

Downstream of Rokeby Park, the Tees enters the lowlands and leaves behind the North Pennines. In doing so, it passes the handsome village of Whorlton, which features another historic river-crossing provided by its ornate suspension bridge (still retaining the former toll-house). When completed in 1831, the bridge was one of the earliest of its type to have a deck supported only by the iron chains and piers. The river continues to be of great charm here, jumping and swirling around a series of waterworn rock shelves, with the rock platforms having in places an unusual chequerboard appearance due to regular jointing in the limestone bedrock. Alas, Whorlton Lido, a former recreation area with miniature railway on the south bank of the river, has now gone. The nearby hamlet of Wycliffe is believed by most authorities to be the birthplace of the reformer and bible-translator John Wyclif, a key figure in the evolution of the English language alongside other such luminaries as Tyndale, Caxton, Shakespeare and the arch-lexicographer Samuel Johnson.

Returning to Barnard Castle and travelling upstream, there is a distinct contrast between the opposite sides of the Tees valley. On the east bank of the river are scattered farmsteads but no villages exist below Eggleston. This was the medieval hunting territory of Shipley Forest and Marwood Chase, with the warden of the forest having his residence at the isolated house of High Shipley. Further eastwards is the quiet secluded valley of *Langleydale*, known to few outside the district, but still retaining its impressive railway viaduct from the disused Barnard Castle to Bishop Auckland line. Downstream along the Langley Beck are the attractive village of Staindrop (with a particularly historic church) and the splendour of Raby Castle with its 19th century façade masking an impressive structure dating back to the 14th century.

On the west bank of the Tees, settlements are more common and a series of tributary valleys branch off from the main valley. The first of these tributary valleys is *Deepdale*, easily passed unnoticed because it is hidden in a narrow wooded dell at Startforth (near Barnard Castle), although its upper course is set amongst bare desolate moors. JBS Morritt took Sir Walter Scott this way on his first visit to Rokeby, both breathlessly clambering up the rocks of Catscastle Crags on horseback. The crags have now been significantly modified by quarrying, but the pleasant woodland falls of Crag Force remain.

The first of the villages is the small row of houses at Lartington, with the dominant building being Lartington Hall, extensively restored in recent decades but with features dating back to the 17th century. This is followed by *Cotherstone*, a larger village grouped around two greens with an array of distinctive Victorian houses. The ancient lords of the manor, the Fitz-Hughs, had their residence at a motte-and-bailey castle on a knoll above the river. Little now remains of their castle: after it was sacked by the Scots it was then raided for building material. At the south end of the village, set on its own, is a Quaker meeting house. The dismantled Tees Valley railway, a branch line that ran from Barnard Castle to Middleton, also had a station here. As a result, the village was very popular for a while with visitors escaping the coalfield towns, even being nicknamed 'Little Sunderland'. Times may have changed, but the village still retains a reputation for its creamy 'Cotherstone Cheese'.

The Tees itself is mainly hidden in fine woodlands in this section: Flatts Wood, Towlerhill Wood, Wilden Wood, Shipley Wood and Great Wood. In spring the woodland floor becomes profusely carpeted with bluebells and garlicky ramsons. At Percymyre Rock, high above Cotherstone, there is a sumptuous panorama of valley and moor from the abrupt cliff-edge. Legend tells that the last of the Fitz-Hugh overlords met his end here during a hunt, falling over the edge in headlong pursuit of prey. On the west bank is Woden Croft, another of the notorious 'Yorkshire Schools' condemned by Charles Dickens in 'Nicholas Nickleby'. A short distance upstream of Percymyre and Woden Croft, there is a particularly impressive scene where the river surges around a sweeping curve, broken by whitewater rapids and stepped shelving falls. In places, hollows have been worn from the sandstone rocks giving this enchanting section the local name of *Fairy Cupboards*.

On the back road leading from Cotherstone to Bowes is the Butter Stone, a legacy from the time of plague, when coins were left in vinegar on the stone to pay for goods. Even such extreme precautions against the risks of personal contact were not always successful. The next village up the valley, *Romaldkirk*, lost many of its inhabitants in 1664 after a local miller contracted the plague on a business trip to Newcastle. Here is perhaps the most characteristic of the Teesdale villages, three spacious greens endowing Romaldkirk with an aura of relaxed distinction. The large church with 15th century tower is a legacy of the prosperous wool and cloth trade, and formerly acted as the focal point for the largest parish in England. The village also had links with lead mining in the dale, the railway station being used to transport the lead pigs from Blackton smelt mill (at Eggleston) to market. This previous bustle of activity was the reason for the village having five inns and a brewery, together with twice-yearly fairs. Nowadays, its continuing attractions mean it is still able to support two of the inns.

The exact status of St. Romald is uncertain, but the most likely candidate is the son of a 9th century Northumbrian prince who in his very short life of three days is reputed to have miraculously declared his Christian faith. Although religious differences have long dissolved, it has been said that the character of some of the Teesdale villages has been inherited from their favoured method of worship: Cotherstone for Quakers, Romaldkirk for church people, Mickleton for primitive Methodists, Middleton for Wesleyans, and so forth.

Romaldkirk

The Tees in spate near the Fairy Cupboards

Blackton Reservoir at Low Birk Hat, Baldersdale

The long side-valley of *Baldersdale* opens out westwards between Cotherstone and Romaldkirk, with the little hamlet of Hunderthwaite near its entrance from the north. Both roads into this dale are dead-ends, there being no through route, leaving a quiet valley becoming gradually more remote as one proceeds higher into its domain. This seclusion did not escape the water planners, however, and Baldersdale has been transformed by three large reservoirs constructed to supply the burgeoning conurbation of Teesside. Blackton and Hury were created at the end of the 19th century with the subsequent valley-head reservoir at Balderhead constructed in the 1960's as a response to anticipated further growth in demand. Along with the lakes in adjacent Lunedale, the reservoirs are now connected to a much larger water transfer system utilising Keilder Water in the north. This system links the catchments of the Tyne, Wear and Tees together with the objective of topping up river levels during periods of low flow.

The reservoirs have not spoiled Baldersdale, although sometimes an ugly tidemark does appear. The scene remains very tranquil, valley pastures being backed by wide spacious moors popular with curlews and other wading birds. At Blackton, beneath the huge earth embankment of Balderhead Reservoir, is the former hostel once catering for Pennine Way walkers. Nearby are the farms of High Birk Hat and Low Birk Hat, the latter indelibly associated with local personality Hannah Hauxwell.

Baldersdale from Shacklesborough

Hannah Hauxwell and Baldersdale

It's my favourite place here ... down the new road through the iron gate. I stand here and watch the seasons come and go. At night the moonlight plays on Hunder Beck .....and the waters sing a song to me .....
Too Long A Winter
Hannah Hauxwell

The name of Baldersdale is now inevitably linked with the personality of Hannah Hauxwell, who lived for many years in difficult circumstances at Low Birk Hat by the Blackton Reservoir. After the early death of her parents, she lived alone at the remote farmhouse, bypassed by modern life. Her main company would usually be a cow that provided a meagre means of income, and which also acted as a 'mobile radiator' in winter, in the absence of other heat sources.

A quirk of fate eventually brought her spartan lifestyle to an incredulous TV audience. With the Pennine Way routed past her doorstep, a passing walker met Hannah and then mentioned the meeting to a friend who produced TV documentaries, observing that she was a good talker and had an amazingly positive outlook on life despite the lack of electricity and running water.

This chain of events eventually led to her appearance in a Yorkshire TV documentary 'Too Long A Winter' that portrayed the harsh lifestyles still prevalent in the northern uplands. Although other people and places were also featured in the documentary, the overwhelming reaction of viewers was to Hannah Hauxwell, and in particular to her stoical attitude and self-sufficient lifestyle. This unanticipated response then brought an unexpected fame in newspaper columns, followed by a series of books on her life and then further TV appearances.

However, despite some improvements in conditions at Low Birk Hat, the long Baldersdale winters and the isolation continued. Eventually, Hannah accepted the inevitable and left the farmhouse to move down the dale to the more amenable location of Cotherstone in 1988. The farm buildings were then sold to be occupied by new owners.

Fortunately, part of the land around Low Birk Hat has now come under the auspices of Durham Wildlife Trust. This has had the happy outcome of becoming 'Hannah's Meadow', where the traditional hay meadow with its abundant wildflowers can continue to flourish. Life in the dale also continues, despite the gradual abandonment of many of the farms in the more marginal locations, as Hannah has recorded in her books. Although the economics of hill-sheep farming are inevitably often rather precarious, it remains as the mainstay of the valley, supporting those farms that still continue to maintain the old traditions.

The flat-topped rocky crowns of Goldsborough and Shacklesborough form distinctive landmarks on the south side of Baldersdale, both capped by gritstone blocks that have weathered more slowly than their surroundings. On closer acquaintance, Goldsborough is particularly distinctive with the cap rocks forming an impressive series of overhangs that roof the hollows worn from the weaker rocks below. One of these features forms the grandly-named Robin Hood's Hole, identified with either the legendary outlaw or more likely the shadowy figure also known as Robin Goodfellow (or 'the Green Man'). The coarse rock and weathered features of the overhangs have also become popular with rock climbers, dating back to the time when Lakeland pioneer and Everest climber Bentley Beetham came here in the 1920s with his Goldsborough Club from Barnard Castle School. One unusual route, albeit short, gains its technical appeal by digital manipulation of a round dimple in the rock that is apparently an old bullet-hole; the military have long gone from here but do still train over on Loup's Hill to the east. Some of the rocks have also been quarried, and there are traces of a sledgate on the north side, with the production of millstones indicated by discarded samples hidden in the long grass.

Near Romaldkirk, the sturdy stone arches of Eggleston Bridge provide one of the limited road crossings over the Tees. A short distance downstream, the integrated Tyne/Wear/Tees aqueduct tunnel from Keilder Water debouches into the Tees: it is normally dry but allows the potential to supplement the river flow when water levels are low. Scattered across the hillside above the bridge is the village of *Eggleston*, dating back to the time of the earliest settlers (when it was Ecgel's settlement), and with a superb prospect up the dale. The prominent Eggleston Hall was designed for William Hutchinson by the Durham architect Ignatius Bonomi in 1820, and the spacious grounds contain interesting walled gardens and the ruins of an 18th century church. On the western fringes of the village are a remarkable series of medieval cultivation terraces, constructed on this slope to maximise the sunny aspect and good drainage, thereby encouraging a better crop harvest.

Higher up the hill, little remains of the Blackton smelt mill, once a major local landmark. The mill was built in 1820 by the London Lead Company to process ore from the local mines and replaced smaller outdated structures nearby. Access to the mill from the west involved packhorses or carts negotiating the deep ravine of Eggleston Burn downstream of where it emerged from the rocky recesses of East Skears gorge: the company eventually alleviated this effort by constructing the high viaduct of Blackton Bridge. At the peak of the lead mining activity, Eggleston's population rose to over 800 but since then it has steadily dropped to less than 300.

The overhangs of Goldsborough above Hury Reservoir

Eggleston Bridge

Ore from the lead mines was also taken east along the 'Steele Road' to the Gaunless Mill, still clearly identifiable by the conspicuous chimney remaining near the village of Copley. This settlement and the adjacent villages of Woodland and Butterknowle stand on the eastern fringe of the Pennines where the lowest seams of the Durham coalfield begin to appear near the surface, so providing plentiful fuel for the smelting hearths at the mill. The crossing of the moors from Eggleston to Woodland is by a little col at the top of Folly Top hill; the col is also cut by a cluster of prominent dry channels left by glacial meltwater forced along this route into the upper Gaunless valley by the pressure of ice in the Tees valley. The River Gaunless probably takes its name from the Norse term for 'useless', a reference to the lack of pasture or fish it provided for the early settlers: it eventually turns north near Bishop Auckland to meet the Wear. Woodland Fell has evidence of prehistoric use from cup-marked rocks and enclosures, with flint arrowheads also being found.

To the north of Eggleston, the head of the Eggleshope valley was one of the richest mining areas in Teesdale. Both branches of the upper valley, Great and Little Eggleshope (the latter followed by the B6278 as it crosses to Weardale), had rich lead veins and several mines exploiting them, as shown by the large spoil heaps, with the Wiregill and Little Eggleshope mines being the most lucrative. Traces of the old leats that brought water power to the mines can be followed along the valley sides in several places, with the route carefully surveyed to ensure the appropriate gradient and maintained by culverts and revetments.

On the south bank of the Tees, *Mickleton* is the last village in the valley before Middleton is reached. Its long linear structure, with houses strung along the road for almost a mile, also reflects the loss of the village green by enclosure. Douglas Ramsden, in his 1947 book on Teesdale, described Mickleton as a 'straggling workaday village that does not invite one to linger' but nowadays with the closure of the nearby quarries its original character has happily re-emerged. The village also marks the junction of Lunedale with the main valley, as indicated by the large viaduct where the Tees Valley Railway crossed the River Lune.

Lunedale is somewhat similar to Baldersdale in that it is dominated by large reservoirs, but differs in that it provides a through route, the B6276 road climbing through the valley to eventually cross to Brough and the Eden valley. Drumlins are prominent in the lower and middle valley, forming a bumpy landscape of undulating ridges, partly flooded by the reservoir waters. Occasionally, the old double-arched bridge at Grassholme, which was replaced by a newer structure when the reservoir was built, resurfaces from below the waters when levels are low. On the northern flanks of the valley are the conspicuous clump of trees on Kirkcarrion and a further series of disused quarries.

Lune Head with T' Big Country beyond

The place-names of Lunedale are redolent of the early Scandanavian settlers: Wemmergill, Thringarth and Selset all being derived from old Norse names. Further up the dale, beyond the isolated farmsteads of Grains o' the Beck and Lune Head, mining was at one time the major activity. The Lunehead and Closehouse mines were the most productive of these workings and together with other passing trade could provide enough business to sustain three inns in the valley. In places, the hillsides are scarred by deep 'hushes', notably around the prominent curricks of The Standards. All the mines have now closed, although barytes was worked at Closehouse until quite recently and some landscape restoration work was required after the opencast excavations.

The expansive open spaces surrounding Lunedale are aptly referred to locally as 'T' Big Country'. A vast unfrequented landscape sweeps from Lune Head Moss up to the crowning ridge-crests of Mickle Fell and Little Fell. Much of this terrain is rather poorly-drained and covered by rough tussock grass or bog, whilst part of it comes under the auspices of the MOD Warcop Range. Undeterred explorers will discover one of the wildest areas of land in the country. Limestone outcrops add occasional features of interest, including swallow holes at Cruckle Pot and John O' Pot, whilst at the remote Arngill Force there is an impressive waterfall and gorge.

Hay meadows, Widdybank

Upper Teesdale

Among the many fine topographers and naturalists associated with the old West Riding, Teesdale was the ultimate goal .... Forever at the backs of their minds as something special.

The Changing Dales, WR Mitchell 1988

Upper Teesdale is a unique landscape of exceptional interest. The quirk of geology that produced the Whin Sill is most pronounced in this part of the Pennines, providing an array of distinctive landforms associated with dramatic scenery. The dale is also endowed with an exceptionally rich flora, varying through the seasons, and adding vivid splashes of colour in the most unlikely places. Most of all, however, it is the character of the River Tees itself that defines the upper dale. Its peat-stained waters rush through an ever-changing combination of foaming cataracts and swirling pools, interspersed with wide strands and rocky islands. The source is the springs of Tees Head, high on Cross Fell, loftiest of the Pennines.

The earliest record of the name is as 'Tese' in the Viking *Knytlinga* saga (1026AD). Due to its propensity for flooding, this aptly translates as the 'boiling or surging river'. Formerly, the river defined the boundary between County Durham and Yorkshire below Cauldron Snout, and remains as the demarcation between the two large estates of Raby and Strathmore. Although sparsely populated, most of the habitations in the dale are on the north bank where the whitewashed buildings on the Raby estate are a prominent feature of the landscape.

Middleton is the 'capital' of the upper dale, and indeed its only settlement of any significant size. It occupies a safe terrace well above the floodplain of the river, conveniently sheltered by hills to the north. Although the origin of the village dates back to the early settlers in the dale, its present structure owes much to the London Lead Company who used it as their headquarters for the district. During the mid-19th century, mining employed 90% of local people, either directly or in support services. At one stage in the 1870s, serious thought was even given to extending the Tees Valley Railway from Barnard Castle through the upper dale to Alston in order to service the numerous mines *en route*. The company's head office was at Middleton House, located at the top of the Hude, above the west end of the village. This was built in 1823 to a design by Ignatius Bonomi and provides a commanding prospect of both village and dale. The Quaker principles of the company directors meant that education was given a high priority in village life: schools, chapels and a reading room were all provided for workers and their families. In addition, Masterman Place and the New Town were constructed as model housing developments. In the centre of the village, the ornamental drinking fountain marks the retirement of Robert Bainbridge, company superintendent, and is similar to that in the other London Lead Company village at Nenthead.

Clock Tower, Middleton

To the south of Middleton, on the broad ridge of Harter Fell between Teesdale and Lunedale, is the prominent clump of trees at Kirkcarrion. Harter Fell is the site of the traditional beacon lit on major festivities such as coronations or jubilees. The walled enclosure at Kirkcarrion marks a tumulus, apparently the burial place of

Caryn, a prince of the Brigantes: excavations here have revealed a Bronze Age urn. Perhaps not surprisingly, there are suggestions that the site is haunted, and the shrouding trees certainly lend the enclosure an eerie aura. Also conspicuous on these slopes are the series of quarries formerly worked for whinstone at Lonton, Crossthwaite and Park End. A small railway line formerly transported the quarried rock from Park End Quarry to the main branch line at Middleton station.

Richard Watson, the 'Teesdale Poet'

Here I may sweat and dig for lead
'Mid smoke and dust, to earn my bread,
And go half clothed and half fed,
Till I can work no more.

Even when judged against the harsh conditions prevalent in the lead-mining communities, Richard Watson had a tough start in life. At the age of 14 he had to take on the responsibility of providing for his mother and eight siblings by working in the mines. Nevertheless, he became one of those who took advantage of the London Lead Company's emphasis on education, and developed a flair for poetry. His lively free-flowing anecdotes and evocative descriptions of working life and festivities, earned 'Poet Dick' the acclaim of his peers, and an important place in the social history of the dale.

One of his best-known poems describes the route from his home at Holwick to work at the distant Little Eggleshope Mine, which he would follow every Monday to lodge at the mine 'shop' during the working week. His route proceeded by Newbiggin then over Hardberry Hill to Coldberry Mine, followed by two more hills past Manorgill Mine to Little Eggleshope. Many of his other poems tell of local stories and morals, or were written to celebrate social functions organized by the company. His most potent words show a deep and abiding affection for the dale and its people. When he had finished with lead mining, he became a labourer but died in 1891, aged 58, following a quarry accident. His grave is in the churchyard of St. Mary's Church at Middleton. Shortly before his death, he composed his own four-verse epitaph, of which the following is the first verse:

The beauties of his native Tees,
The rocks, and dells, and stately trees,
And cataracts grand; such scenes as these
His soul admired.
They were like sermons, and with ease
His muse inspired.

Kirkcarrion from Bowbank

Hudeshope valley with Coldberry Mine on the left

North of Middleton is the side valley of *Hudeshope*. In its lower reaches this is attractively wooded with the popular path of the King's Walk and a short section of minor road leading by the stream past the Horseshoe Falls. At the road terminus are the excellently-preserved kilns built by the Parker family to produce lime from nearby quarries hidden in the trees. Above this point, Hudeshope Beck emerges from the recesses of the deep Skears gorge overlooked by the sheer limestone cliffs of Jack Scar. Close to the foot of the cliffs is a small cave on the east bank, recognisable by the resurgent stream; in his autobiographical account of local life back in the 19th century, Tom Todd described boyhood adventures in this cave, exploring its dank passages by candlelight.

Beyond the Skears gorge and reached either by the valley path or narrow roads on either side, the upper part of the Hudeshope valley is a complete contrast to the lower section. Mining has had a profound influence on the landscape, with major workings at Coldberry, Lodge Sike, Low Skears and High Skears leaving substantial remains. Extensive tracts of spoil on the east side of the valley mark Lodge Sike Mine, but the largest of the subterranean workings was at Coldberry Mine, high up on the western slopes, and clearly distinguished by the deep 'hush' ravine of Coldberry Gutter. A particular feature of this mine was the water-balance system used to raise a tub of ore up the main shaft, using as a counter-balance a tub of water moving down a railed incline. Coldberry Mine finally closed in 1956, after operating for more than 200 years. The main building remaining today is the large lodging-house of Coldberry Shop, recently restored by the North Pennines Heritage Trust. Despite the influence of the London Lead Company, conditions at the mine were harsh, especially when its economics became more marginal. In 1890, washer boys went on strike for more pay, which brought the mine to a standstill, and a little later in 1896 two boys were killed when working the wastes, due to a collapse of debris.

The main valley of the Tees between Middleton and Langdon Beck is justly celebrated for its wonderful river scenery and flowery meadows. By popular accolade, it is usually considered the most beautiful section of the Pennine Way. A regular flow of day-walkers on the valley path also helps to maintain the shuttle minibus service up the dale. This service is the modern equivalent of the 'Teesdale Queen' bus that transported dalesfolk to market in Middleton during the day and to its lively dances during the evening. In its early course, the valley path passes Park End Wood, a surviving remnant of the old forest that formerly covered the dale, providing a mix of oak, ash and alder. Nearby, only scattered stones mark the forgotten buildings of Unthank: in a district once rife with superstition, the ruins were said to be haunted by a bogle, the traditional bogeyman of young children throughout northern England.

Parker's Kilns

Skears Bridge

The Upper Teesdale Flora

Although there are other areas of the North Pennines containing an unusual flora, Upper Teesdale is undoubtedly pre-eminent in this regard. Three distinctive habitats, in particular, have earned it recognition at national and international levels of significance. Firstly, the hay meadows which are traditionally cut in late summer allowing ample time for a greater herb-rich diversity of species than modern farming methods would normally tolerate. A particular Teesdale speciality of these 'herby meadows' is the yellow globeflower (aptly referred to locally as 'double-dumplings'). The second important habitat is often referred to as 'turfy pastures' and is found on irregular terrain such as drumlin ridges and other glacial deposits that have been used as valley intakes for ranging livestock. These pastures typically have a high water table with frequent lime-rich springs and flushes. Species such as alpine bartsia, spring gentian and marsh orchid are often unusually common here. The third habitat occurs on the fells where thin *rendzina* soils on isolated outcrops of 'sugar limestone', or rocky outcrops of unaltered limestone have provided *refugia* for arctic-alpine rarities including spring gentian, Teesdale violet, mountain avens and alpine forget-me-not.

The presence of the unusual arctic-alpine species is a result of the unique conjunction of geology and climate in the dale. This has allowed flowers from the end of the last ice age to persist, whilst elsewhere they have been replaced by trees and common grasses. At the key localities, the geology has produced atypical soils that are often thin and lime-rich discouraging tree growth, and sometimes also with a high lead content. In addition, the upland setting has continued to retain its harsh climate which, when combined with the unfavourable mineral content of the soils, has meant that common grasses are rather unproductive. The end result is distinctive ecological niches that specialist plants have continued to occupy, whilst those of their surroundings have changed. A particularly unusual survival is dwarf birch, which has a very isolated colony in a bog amongst the heather: conditions in the bog must have remained conducive to its presence despite the major changes around it over the last 10,000 years.

Much of the dale has been designated as a protected conservation area to conserve the rare habitats and species. Most notably, the combined Upper Teesdale and Moor House National Nature Reserve covers a large swathe of the upper valley and high ground, with a programme of ongoing research into ecology and management. The hay meadows and pastures are also sustained by grant-aid to encourage traditional farming methods. This maintains the production of hay rather than early-year silage, and encourages appropriate stocking levels together with a lack of chemical spraying, artificial fertilisers or grass-seed sowing.

Spring gentian

The Early Botanists

The discovery of the Upper Teesdale flora owes much to the enthusiasm of local botanists in the early 19th century. The most well-known of these individuals were the Quaker father and son, both named James Backhouse, who were expert chroniclers of the flora and helped to bring the dale to wider notice. However, in their writings, they acknowledged that many of the important finds had in fact been made by John Binks, a local miner who supplemented his income by scouring the fells for plants of medicinal value (such as rose-root or juniper).

In addition, recent research tends to confirm that the local apothecary, William Oliver, was a very significant figure in the discoveries by recognising the importance and rarity of many of the unusual species. As elsewhere, the clergy were also enthusiastic amateurs, particularly John Harriman, curate of Eggleston and Gainford. At a much earlier stage, some important initial finds in the dale were recorded in the late 17th century by Ralph Johnson, vicar of Brignall.

Winch Bridge

Low Force

A particularly sublime section of the river occurs between Scoberry Bridge and the Winch Bridge, where the river dashes over a series of rapids between dark rock columns. In spring and summer, the banks become a carpet of wild flowers and the lush meadows contrast with a series of variegated woodlands on the north side. Amongst the riverside rocks, yellow splashes of shrubby cinquefoil are particularly distinctive in June and July. A feature of the river is its multiplicity of channels as the river diverges around columnar blocks and islands of whinstone: in normal conditions, many of these routes are scarcely utilised, but in spate the river surges through all available avenues at breakneck speed.

At the Winch Bridge, the arrangement of features reaches perfection, with the river flowing through a narrow gorge headed by the picturesque double fall of *Low Force*. A footbridge was first strung across the gorge in 1704 to allow miners from Holwick village to gain access to the Redgrove and Pikelaw mines on the opposite side. The bridge was formed by two long chains which had a series of wooden planks fixed across them and it was supported by shorter chains attached to each bank, with a rather limited handrail. This early origin gives it a strong claim as the first suspension bridge in Europe. The original rickety structure collapsed during 1802 in tragic circumstances when a large and merry haymaking party seems to have overloaded the supports, and two people were lost in the deep waters below. The present bridge dates from 1830 and has had more recent modifications to further reinforce the structure. Although now more structurally sound, the recent adjustment work has alas largely removed the amiable 'wobble' that used to be experienced!

Both banks of the river allow differing views of the falls, and thereby provide a full appreciation of their colourful surroundings. In places, the erosive power of the river has scoured out pitted holes in the river bed through the swirling action of pebbles. The old name of Salmon Leap indicates that the falls were also once a notable obstacle in the upstream passage of these fish when they swarmed in profusion up the river in the days before industry brought pollution to its lower reaches.

On the north bank, near to Low Force, are the hamlets of Newbiggin and Bowlees, located just off the main road up the dale. The whitewashed farms and other buildings harmonize perfectly with their surroundings of patchwork pastures, stone walls, field barns and tree-lined streams. Newbiggin chapel, built in 1760, is believed to be the oldest surviving Methodist building that has remained in continuous use. Meanwhile, the disused chapel at nearby Bowlees has been thoughtfully converted into a visitor centre, providing one of the most popular sites in the dale. The sparkling cascades of Pasture Beck above Newbiggin provide another hidden delight.

Gibson's Cave

Hell Cleugh

A short walk on a well-worn path alongside the stream at Bowlees leads to the interesting waterfall of Summerhill Force. As often occurs, the resistant rim of the fall protrudes as a lip, but in this case a large cavern has been eroded in the softer rocks under the overhang to its right. This is *Gibson's Cave*, legendary hideaway of a local outlaw and an impressive illustration of the selective powers of erosion on different rock types. In summer, the old quarries by the path provide another colourful display of local flowers. The path to the cave is very popular, but a little higher up the Bow Lee Beck is a much less frequented and wilder scene at the confluence of the Wester Beck and Flushiemere Beck. Both streams have each carved deep ravines, with the tree-shrouded gorge of the latter forming the impressive Hell Cleugh.

Mining remains are very conspicuous on the northern slopes of the valley. Above Newbiggin are the remains of mines at Pasture Burn and Redgroves, with the fellside being gouged by the wide gash of Red Grooves Hush. The 'hush' forms a pronounced nick on the skyline and actually cuts right through the watershed, complementing Coldberry Gutter on the other side. Water to scour out these channels was supplied by the Whistle Jacket Reservoir on the moor above, named apparently after one of the Earl of Northumberland's favourite racehorses.

Even more remarkable are the upper slopes of the Flushiemere Beck, where the extensive use of 'hushes' at Pikelaw has completely altered the natural contours (photo: p.3), representing probably the most intensive use of this mining technique in the North Pennines. The 'hushes' and shafts probably date from the 18th century but later, levels were driven to explore the ground and some barytes was extracted in the 20th century. The prominent building at Flushiemere Mine Shop is now a ruin but once had 26 beds crammed into it, each of which could sleep two or three men. A minor road to Weardale passes above Flushiemere Beck following the old packhorse route across the watershed at Swinhope Head. To the west, Ettersgill Common is one of the traditional sites where black grouse can be seen displaying and competing for territory in the 'lek'.

Throughout this section of the dale, the dark whinstone crags of Holwick Scar form a prominent feature on its south side. Below its shattered columns and broad scree slopes, the hamlet of *Holwick* is strung out along an adjacent ridge. A narrow little valley lies between houses and crags, at the head of which parts of the Scar have become detached and eroded into the impressive turret-shaped remnants of The Castles. Where streams descend to meet the Scar, they are diverted into a series of stepped cascades through rocky channels, producing Crag Scar Force and the charming niche of the Fairy Dell above Mill Beck Wood. These were favourite locations of Richard Watson, the 'Teesdale Poet', who lived at Holwick and featured them in his verses.

Above Low Force, the river scenery continues in similar style to Holwick Head Bridge, where the river is seen to emerge from a deep gorge. A short distance further up the river and the reason for the gorge is soon revealed, the roar of water reaching a crescendo, often with sheets of dancing spray, at the magnificent spectacle of *High Force*. Most visitors to this famous landmark use the short toll path from the hotel on the north bank, but the path on the south side, after passing through a remarkable area of juniper scrub, provides a more complete view of the scene. The formation of High Force is one of the more spectacular consequences of the Whin Sill, which here cuts across the course of the river, providing rocks more resistant than the underlying limestone. The river has then steadily eroded backwards through the discontinuity to form the gorge, leaving the fall at its current position with a deep plunge pool carved in the rocks below by the explosive force of the falling water.

When the river level is high, a second fall appears from a channel to the right of the main fall, and an island develops between the two at the top. This island has a history of trapping unwary visitors and has been the scene of several perilous rescues. During one of these events in 1880, a sudden summer storm ensnared two men on the central column: in the ensuing rescue attempt, one of the victims was swept to his death whilst the other was eventually retrieved by rope. In full flood conditions, much less prevalent now due to the building of Cow Green Reservoir, the middle island also becomes engulfed and both channels merge into a awesome torrent, thundering over the falls into a maelstrom of white water and spray. In the past, old photographs show High Force as frozen into solid ice, but those days seem to have gone now, the last time this being recorded was in 1929.

Rather incongruously situated above High Force is the large active works of Dine Holme Quarry, extracting the same hard whinstone rock (for use in road-metal) that has produced the waterfall. The contrast with the riverside scenery could hardly be more pronounced, but fortunately the immediate prospect is redeemed by the fine double-fall of Bleabeck Force, where a tributary stream dashes down the fellside to reach the parent river. Above the scars of the quarry, the rocky knolls and juniper woods of Force Garth form an interesting landscape that marks the entrance into the higher parts of the valley. Traces of early occupation have been found at both Force Garth (a Romano-British settlement from about 1st century AD) and across the river at Bracken Rigg (probably dating from the Bronze Age). This section of the dale is still known as Forest-in-Teesdale, harking back to the time when it was a hunting preserve. The parish name is Forest and Frith, the 'frith' being the protected area set apart for the young deer, and the nearby buildings of Dirt Pit have inherited their name from a corrupted translation of the original 'deer path'.

Holwick Scar

High Force

Bleabeck Force

The scattered whitewashed farmsteads of *Langdon Beck* lie in a distinct upland setting that contrasts with the gentle valley pastures further down the dale. Here the intake fields are interspersed with rougher ground and rocky irregularities, somewhat restricting the options for farming. Undulations formed by ice-streamed drumlins have resulted in a series of long ridges parallel with the valley, separated by marshy hollows. In spring these hollows become a yellow sea of marsh marigolds, and migrating birds return from their winter haunts to occupy favoured sites amongst the rushes and long grass. Particularly visible are the floppy-winged erratic swoops of the lapwing but in audible terms the scene is usually much more varied including the drumming of snipe or the *tirr-pee-you* calls of the golden plover, as well as the familiar *tewitt-tewitt* of the lapwing.

On the fell above Langdon Beck is the prominent escarpment of High Hurth Edge. This contains an interesting cave system of archaeological significance, traditionally referred to as *Moking Hurth*, but in the past known as the Fairy Hole and in times before that as the Hobthrush Hole (photo: p.14). Lime-working has modified the outer sections of the caves, but the innards consist of narrow entrances dropping to passageways with a wider base than their slit-like upper sections. Narrow transverse joints link laterally across the main passages, with a notional through-route from a swallow-hole on the plateau above. Excavations in the cave bed have revealed over 30 animal species from this site, including lynx and wolf, and also a human skull and skeleton dated at about 3000 years old. Finds from the fields below the cave also imply a long history of use and suggest that the site was occupied for a considerable length of time. The lack of dense tree cover on the thin limestone soils and the availability of shelter would have been the primary attractions. On the nearby hills, flint arrow-heads have been found on Holwick Fell, Green Fell and Cronkley Fell. The prominent stone-men cairns on the fell above Moking Hurth mark the site of old quarry workings at Chapel Bowers, used for local building material and part of a system of workings extending westwards to the larger excavations of 'ganister' sandstone at Harthope Bank.

At Langdon Beck, the road to Alston (B6277) leaves the main valley of the Tees and climbs by the upland hollow of the Harwood Beck to its summit at Yad Moss (so named because the thickness of peat is a yard or more). The settlement of *Harwood-in-Teesdale* is a scattering of farmsteads and other buildings in this secluded valley. These hill farms are amongst the most elevated in the country, and one of the smallholdings at 600m once had a good claim to be its highest habitation. However, the growing season is short and the upper pastures were always marginal: their abandonment means that only the lower valley floor is now farmed.

Forest-in-Teesdale and Cronkley Scar

Harwood dale

White Force and Black Arc Mine

Several mines were scattered around the Harwood valley, some being very productive, notably at the Lady's Rake site. Other mining trials were less profitable, with the array of old shafts and hushes above Ashgill Head and Grasshill indicating that the 'Old Man' had already thoroughly explored this ground. Lady's Rake Mine had an innovative water balance system to raise ore in a similar way to that which was used at Coldberry Mine in the Hudeshope valley. The sad ruins of St. James' Church at Harwood indicate the substantial depopulation of this area: its walled enclosure has been used to suggest a very early ecclesiastical site here.

Nevertheless, despite the inevitable changes over time, farming life at Harwood does continue. In late summer, hay-making remains the focus of activity with the grass cut and dried to maximise winter fodder resources depending on the prevailing weather of that year. Previously, the hay would be heaped into 'cocks' or 'rucks' to accelerate the drying process, and when stored in the barn some rushes would be added on top to absorb any remaining moisture. Recently, one of the Harwood farms at Herdship has won particular acclaim for the quality of its produce, and the valley is still renowned for the rich flora of its hay meadows, including the celebrated spring gentian.

Across the Tees from Langdon Beck is the lone farmstead of Cronkley, safely situated on a high terrace above the river, which in flood occasionally spills out in a wide ribbon across its lower slopes. Frowning over the scene are the broken cliffs and dark screes of Cronkley Scar, another outcrop of the Whin Sill. Hidden below the Scar, and unsuspected from most viewpoints, is the small lake of Tarn Dub, impounded by a smooth moraine ridge. The inference is that a small glacier may have survived here, nourished mainly by blown snow from above, when the main valley had become ice-free. In a little cove to the left of the main section of cliffs is the long cascade of White Force above the ruins of the old Black Arc mine. The waterfall is unusual, falling over a cliff formed by the dark whinstone to then disappear, in all but the wettest conditions, down a hole dissolved through the fretted limestone below: the subterranean water eventually gushes to the surface again at Cawbank Spring 400m away.

The broad track passing White Force and climbing onto Cronkley Fell is the 'Green Trod', a section of the old cattle-droving route linking Birkdale and Holwick. The flat-topped plateau of Cronkley Fell is renowned amongst naturalists for its crumbly granular outcrops of 'sugar limestone', several of which have been fenced off to protect them from grazing animals, particularly rabbits. Fortunately, the flora still flourishes, and a visit in springtime can be a particularly rewarding experience. At White Well, a small stream surges to the surface in translucent pools set amongst windswept dwarf shrubs; this spring must have provided a welcome source of refreshment for the cattle and horses on the Green Trod. On a clear day, the view from Cronkley Fell is superb: it sweeps around from the nearby slopes of Mickle Fell to the headwaters of Maize Beck and the Tees amongst the highest tops of the Pennines; the swarthy fells contrasting with the tidy pastures and homely buildings of the valley floor.

On the slopes of Mickle Fell are further traces of old workings from the Silverband and Green mines, together with a series of artificial channels etched into the fellside, notably Birkdale Hush. The miners would have been billeted at the remote buildings of Silverband Shop and Millings Shop.

Both Mickle Fell and its neighbour Little Fell are now more renowned for their arctic-alpine flora, but access to them is rather problematic as both fells are located within the 'Danger Area' of the Warcop artillery range. Mickle Fell formerly had the distinction of being the highest point in Yorkshire and it now has the equivalent status within County Durham. It forms a long elevated ridge that, as with neighbouring Little Fell, is mainly composed of limestone, overlaid by a small gritstone cap at the summit. Amongst the limestone blocks on its upper slopes can be found abundant fossils of crinoids. The presence of lime on both fells means they rise as green 'islands' above the surrounding blanket bogs, explaining not only the rare flora but also the frequent unexpected density of grazing sheep and moles on these higher slopes.

The unusual and distinctive 'sugar limestone' outcrops and flora of Cronkley Fell are mirrored across the valley on Widdybank Fell. Tucked in between the two fells are Widdybank farm buildings, where the river valley narrows and the 'turfy pastures' extending from Langdon Beck reach their upvalley limit. These pastures occupy a series of irregular bumps and hollows on drumlin ridges, providing a rich pageant of rare flowers in spring and early summer. Particularly lush growths occur around springs where the minerals are concentrated, producing conspicuous 'flushes'.

The pasture land is managed as part of the Upper Teesdale nature reserve with the ecological research suggesting that some form of light disturbance favours the specialist flora by breaking up the ground and providing potential new sites to colonise. In the past, this disturbance role may have been served by grazing aurochs, ancestor of the domestic ox, but now a herd of galloway cattle roam the in-bye land as part of the management system. Favourable disturbance also occurs where the Tees and Langdon Beck have carved their courses into some of the drumlin ridges, creating unstable slopes that occasionally slump downwards, carrying loosely-attached rafts of turf with them. Where the appropriate balance between erosion and stability of the riverbank exists, flowers such as spring gentian and birds-eye primrose can flourish.

The 'Green Trod', Cronkley Fell

Ruined shepherd's hut, Mickle Fell

Cauldron Snout

Upstream of Widdybank farm, the Tees curves around the stony reaches of Holmwath to pass the columnar whinstone crags of Falcon Clints. This impressive place is often further enhanced by the *kek-kek-kek* call and swooping dives of the resident peregrines themselves. Around the curve, at the western end of Falcon Clints, is the magnificent cataract of *Cauldron Snout*. The name captures the scene superbly, with the river spilling over a rocky lip and hurtling down a narrow confined channel in leaps and bounds, before finally fanning out in one final cascade at its foot. The confinement of the channel also allows a level of intimacy not usually found with great waterfalls: at time the water seems playful and mesmerising, but in times of flood there is an awesome fury in the thundering torrent. Old photographs show that a small bridge was once positioned across the cataract, but this was lost in 1925 and replaced by the current structure beyond the top of the falls. Legend says that on moonlit nights, you may hear or see the 'Singing Lady', the spirit of a young woman that, on losing her lover, threw herself into the turbulent waters.

Above Cauldron Snout, the exhilaration of the natural landscape is tempered somewhat by the concrete dam of Cow Green Reservoir. Before the area was flooded by the reservoir in 1971, the river flowed through a broad shallow basin characterised by the languid arc and deep pools of The Weel, a prelude to the drama of the falls. The flooding of the basin will always be shrouded in controversy because here was one of the key habitats of the unique Teesdale flora. Despite efforts at transplanting, much of the habitat was lost when the reservoir was created. The lake has a depth of 23m at its deepest point and can store 40,000 million litres of water but industrial decline has meant that the expected demand for water has not materialised. With the construction of Keilder Water in North Tynedale and aqueducts linking the Tyne-Wear-Tees catchments, the region actually has over-capacity. On the positive side, the new lake does often alleviate the bleakness of the surroundings, acting as a reflecting bowl to soften the scene, with migrant birds also finding sanctuary on its surface. However, with hindsight, the decision to construct a reservoir here seems short-sighted and the environmental damage unnecessary.

The access road to the dam from the car park at Weel Sike means that the walk to Cauldron Snout is often popular. The same road also continues beyond the dam, over the bridge above the falls, leading to the lonely farm of Birkdale, one of the most remote habitations in the Pennines. Back in the 18th century, a retired miner called Anson took advantage of the isolation to establish his own illicit whisky distillery at the farm. During the severe winter of 1947, when there were two farms at Birkdale, two-thirds of the sheep flock were lost. The isolated buildings are now on the route followed by the Pennine Way into the desolate upper reaches of Maize

Beck, passing the impressive waterworn gorge of Maizebeck Scar before crossing the watershed to the drama of High Cup Nick.

> ### The 'Tees Roll'
>
> The large upland catchment of the Tees is extensively covered with thick deposits of peat and therefore acts like an enormous sponge, soaking up water until it reaches saturation and then suddenly releasing it. The excess water flows swiftly into streams, then the river, causing a rapid rise in water levels and a surge of floodwater downvalley. These are the conditions favouring formation of the notorious 'Tees Roll', a wave of water that would thunder down the river, sweeping away all before it. Nowadays, regulation of the headwaters at Cow Green has tamed the river to some extent, and such a 'flood pulse' is much less likely. Although the river certainly retains its capacity to flood, it is not quite with the same ferocity or frequency that occurred previously. Nevertheless, large tributaries such as Maize Beck and Langdon Beck remain unchecked, and especially during rapid snow-melt conditions when the buffering capacity of the reservoir can be exceeded, the river does sometimes run wild again. At such times, the valley sides become ribboned with white horse-tails as previously insignificant streams gush out of the ground and rush down to supplement the raging torrent of the river.
>
> The surge of the 'Tees Roll' has a long history of catching out the unaware due to the sudden rise in river levels. This misfortune has occurred not only at locations such as High Force in the upper dale, but much further downstream on the lowland plains, such as near Barnard Castle and Darlington. In the folklore of the dale, the bubbly river-foam warned of this malevolence: Peg Powler's suds were the sign of a malicious sprite that washed her green clothes in the river and lured feckless children to their fate.

Fortunately, the reservoir did not destroy all of the rare habitats hereabouts. The 'sugar limestone' areas on the upper parts of Widdybank Fell are well above the waters and continue to support a rich flora. Even here, however, there may be subtle threats: there is evidence that the reservoir has changed the local microclimate with the air temperature being about 1°C higher than the adjacent fell, an effect of the different thermal capacity of water compared to the land. Near the Weel Sike car park are the remains of the Cow Green mine. The public road ends at the car park but Peghorn Lane continues above the reservoir to the ruined Dubby Sike mine and then to the old Green Hurth lead mine. Although the lead content was low, both Cow Green and Dubby Sike were worked for barytes until the 1950s, with an aerial ropeway transporting material to Langdon Beck.

Cauldron Snout and an overflowing Cow Green Dam

The 'last homely house', Birkdale farm

Cross Fell and its satellites dominate the headwaters of the Tees, with the radar station on Great Dun Fell usually overtly conspicuous. The only other remaining human edifice in this vast upland swathe is Moor House, formerly a mining structure dating from 1842 and then used as a hunting lodge. Now the building is associated with the large nature reserve covering this area; the warden did once live at the house with his family, but they were 'snowed in' from 21st December 1979 to 21st April 1980, and soon after moved to the Eden valley. An access road from South Tynedale reaches Moor House over the col at Tyne Head, but there is no direct link with Teesdale.

Cow Green Reservoir

Cross Fell from Yad Moss

These remote uppermost reaches of the dale represent another area that seems desolate and wild now, but was much more frequented in the past. In close vicinity, Netherhearth, Teesside, Metalband and Crookburn mines were all extensively worked at various stages, with steam engines being installed to assist the pumping of water. At nearby Tyne Head were the Tynegreen mines, and a water leat was constructed to take water from the Tees over the short distance of moor to serve those mines. It is interesting to note that if this leat had been extended a little further then it would have diverted the headwaters of the Tees into the upper feeder streams of the South Tyne!

Upper Teesdale from Chapel Bowers

The dimpled rocks of Maizebeck Scar

THE NORTH PENNINES

Upper Weardale near Ireshopeburn

Weardale

... from the top of an enormous mountain we had a view of Weardale. It is a lovely prospect: the green gently rising meadows and fields, on both sides of the river as clear as crystal, were sprinkled all over with innumerable little houses.

John Wesley, 1750

Seen from many distant viewpoints, John Wesley's colourful vision of Weardale has much relevance even now. The meadows and green fields are still there, and the curve of the dale between the distant fells remains a handsome prospect. However, in many regards, this is the 'Cinderella' dale of the North Pennines, with a deep hidden beauty. In several places, the scenery is characterised by a considerable legacy left by long-term human exploitation of the landscape. Wesley's description also hints at the reason for this: the 'innumerable little houses' imply a higher than normal population density, which was the result of planned settlement and the steady growth of local industry. Mining and quarrying have certainly left their mark, with the excavations in some areas continuing until quite recently to leave harsh unnatural scars that are gradually beginning to heal. The Bishop of Durham, as the main landowner, has historically been a very influential figure in the dale, by controlling the development of settlements and reserving land for deer parks at Wolsingham and Stanhope.

Despite the ravages of industry, Weardale has certainly retained its considerable charm and has a wealth of interest. The river-name appears to be associated with the Celtic words 'Uisura' or 'Gweir', implying that this is the valley of the 'bending river'. Many side-valleys or 'hopes' branch off from the dale and sometimes have their own attractive scenery. Towards the head of the main valley, the combination of river and pastoral scenery is akin to parts of the Yorkshire Dales. In other places, the blending of a man-made landscape with natural reclamation has produced its own distinctive scene. Furthermore, the logistics of extracting, processing and transporting the mined or quarried material has left some fascinating relics, including the remains of the highest standard-gauge railway in the country.

The town of *Wolsingham* is well-positioned at the entrance to the dale, with origins dating back to Anglo-Saxon times when it was named as Wulfsige's village. It then became a manor of the Bishop of Durham and, following a charter awarded in 1508, developed into an important market town, particularly known for its trade in cattle. An annual agricultural show held in September still remains as a significant event in the Weardale calendar. The old part of the town retains its interesting medieval street pattern, with the houses grouped around the triangle-shaped market place, whilst the demesne area is now a popular leisure venue for townsfolk. The many historic buildings in the old town also lend an aura of distinction, including the 17th and 18th century houses of Whitfield Place and the terrace of old stone houses at West End. A strong Roman Catholic tradition, which survived the turbulence of the Reformation, is still evident in the old grammar school buildings and dedicated church.

Church of St. Mary & St. Stephen, Wolsingham

Tunstall Reservoir

Wolsingham steelworks were established by Charles Attwood in the mid-19th century when he moved the base for his Weardale Iron Company to this location from Tow Law, superseding a previous ironworks. Attwood was an associate of Henry Bessemer, and the emerging new technology for steel-making allowed the business to carry out expeditious casting of a variety of industrial components, including rails and wagon wheels. At the start of the 20th century the business employed over 400 men, evolving into a specialist supplier of ship parts, but then gradually declining as markets became more irregular and uncertain. Charles Attwood also built the magnificent mansion of Holywood Hall on the hillside to the north overlooking the town.

The expanding railway network reached Wolsingham in 1847 with the station being located over the sturdy steel bridge across the river from the town. The valley railway remains functional today with occasional passenger trains running to and from Stanhope, sometimes hauled by steam engines on special occasions. The long-term vision for the line also aims to eventually restore the connecting service with Bishop Auckland (this section of line has been 'mothballed' but not dismantled), although tourism rather than freight is now the principal driver in any assessment of economic viability. The remainder of the Wear Valley line, which once extended beyond the former cement works at Eastgate up to the top of the valley at Wearhead (see page 89), has been dismantled and is therefore probably lost to posterity.

Waskerley Beck flows through Wolsingham to join the Wear, forming the pleasant small falls of The Sills. The side valley from which the beck originates was formerly a park belonging to the Bishop of Durham, and several of the buildings here, such as Fawnlees, Bishop Oak and Baal Hill, have foundations going back to those times. Baal Hill House was the home of the bailiff of the hunting park and has the remains of an advanced bastle design including a vaulted basement. Forester's Lodge also has links with the past, but the present-day building is actually a newer structure, with the original being destroyed when the valley was flooded for a new reservoir in 1880.

Tunstall Reservoir was constructed to supply the Durham coalfield towns and, complemented by its attractive mix of deciduous and coniferous woodlands, has become a popular visitor venue. The reservoir lake attracts a range of wildlife and the woodlands provide very pleasant walking around its perimeter. Fine woodlands are a feature of much of the lower Waskerley valley, with ancient oakwoods at Baal Hill Wood and Backstone Bank Wood. The small valley of Thornhope Beck, to the west, also has the attractive Ladley Wood. Higher up the valley, in a moorland setting at the head of the catchment, another dam has been constructed to impound the waters of Waskerley Reservoir.

William Morley Egglestone

Born in 1838 at Huntshieldford, near St. John's Chapel, Morley Egglestone followed the conventional dalesman's path into the local mines at an early age. However, motivated by the collective eagerness for self-improvement that characterised many mining partnerships, he left the mines in his twenties to set up a shop and small printing press, eventually becoming correspondent for several newspapers. Over the years, he also became a key figure in local government, serving time as a council official, officer for the Poor Rate Union and district sanitary inspector. In the latter position he suggested many improvements to the local water supply and sewerage system. He was also a major advocate for the extension of the valley railway to Wearhead.

Egglestone's abiding interest and fascination remained with the Weardale landscape and this resulted in the publication of numerous articles and books, capturing the many aspects of the dale including its social history, flora and fauna, archaeology and geology. With the major changes occurring in the area through the 20th century, these now form a valuable archive. One of the most interesting of his books has since been updated by Peter Bowes in 1996 and republished as 'Picturesque Weardale Revisited'.

Tunstall Reservoir

Knitsley Fell, looking west

Blackling Hole, Hamsterley Forest

To the south of Wolsingham, Knitsley Fell represents the last of the declining uplands before the transition into lowland pastures and other cultivated land. The fell retains an attractive mixed remnant of heath and woodland, with a superb view of the dale and its surroundings. By the River Wear below Knitsley Fell is Bradley Hall, a notable example of a fortified medieval house with vaulted chambers and moat. At one stage it was the home of the Tempest family who supported the unsuccessful 'Rising of the North' against Elizabeth I, and were therefore removed from their position of power.

Further south again from Knitsley Fell is the valley of the Bedburn Beck which is notable for the large-scale plantations and sylvan delights of *Hamsterley Forest*. In this valley can also be traced the remains of a Romano-British settlement at The Castles and of small-scale iron processing from a bloomery at Bedburn. On a ridge above the valley is the charming village of Hamsterley, originally established as an Anglo-Saxon planned settlement in the old forest (its name meaning the 'clearing of the corn-weevils').

Hamsterley Forest

The afforestation of Hamsterley Common began in 1927, when the estate was acquired by the Forestry Commission, and much of the area is now covered with large plantations. Modern forestry has often been criticised for producing dense blocks of gloomy conifers but Hamsterley Forest provides an excellent example of the benefits accruing from good forest management. Remnants of old woodland have been subtly incorporated into the new plantations, most notably by the banks of streams. This has resulted in a surprisingly varied landscape with over sixty species of trees present, including a flourishing beechwood at Pennington Plantation that is one of the highest in the country. Tracts of heath also exist within the forest boundaries providing a rich crop of bilberries for the discerning palate. Amongst the range of wildlife that has found sanctuary in the forest are the distinctive crossbill and woodpecker.

The forest provides an array of excellent trails, whether followed on foot or by cycle or horseback. On the rare occasions when significant snowfalls blanket the forest, the exhilaration of cross-country ski-ing can also be enjoyed along the same network of tracks. In summer, the secluded wooded glades and sparkling pools can provide a welcome escape from the heat of the day. The key element of the forest is therefore its diversity, and by developing this aspect rather than blindly adopting a monoculture single-species approach, the Forestry Commission have created an important environmental as well as an economic asset.

Continuing up Weardale, the next village is *Frosterley* which has a 13th century origin, possibly founded upon an earlier settlement that was established at this location. The oldest parts of the village are at its eastern end around the small green, where the naming of Pinfold House indicates one of the original uses for a village green, to retain and control livestock. Over time, Frosterley developed to become the centre for the most intensive quarrying industry within the North Pennines, and therefore housed many of the quarrymen. The scale of the industry meant that as one quarry excavation finished in the surrounding area, then another would begin, meaning that in the vicinity of Frosterley there are now the stark remains of ten worked-out quarries.

At about this location in the dale, there is a distinct westwards change in the naming of streams from 'beck' to 'burn'. This distinction reflects a change in influence from the Norse settlers (who had occupied Bishop Auckland but did not penetrate far into Weardale, except at a few isolated sites) to that of the Anglo-Saxon 'Northumbrians' who occupied much of the lowlands and later became established in the northern dales.

The Bollihope Burn is one of the largest tributaries of the Wear, reaching the main valley near Frosterley. Throughout the Bollihope valley much of the original landscape has been extensively modified by human activities, most notably by quarrying. At Broadwood, near the confluence with the Wear, ironstone was worked from a series of small lead veins. Most of the quarries, however, were sources of limestone which after extraction was then processed for a variety of different uses including agricultural lime, cement, concrete, roadstone, and as a flux for steel production. The long row of kilns that remain near Bishopley demonstrates the intensive nature of the lime production that took place in this area, with further kilns also built upstream by the Fine Burn. Harehope Quarry was also the prime site for the renowned 'Frosterley marble', a distinctive local rock that was used within many important buildings, most notably in Durham Cathedral.

A mineral railway, branching off the main valley railway, was constructed alongside the Bollihope Burn to serve the quarries. Above Bishopley, a large cutting was blasted through the solid rock to take the line through to the upper valley. A little higher, at Bollihope Mill, are the ruins of a crushing and smelting mill for processing lead ore. The unusual terrace of houses standing at nearby Hill End, situated on a ridge high above the Wear valley, was built for the smelters and quarry workers. The lead mines established in the Bollihope valley included the productive Cornish Hush and Yew Tree mines that were operated by the London Lead Company in the 19th century. The mines were later worked for fluorspar in the 20th century.

Frosterley 'marble'

A polished limestone rather than a genuine marble, this distinctive rock became much in demand from the 13th century onwards, by providing a local alternative to the famous Purbeck stone of southern England (as used, for example, in Westminister Abbey). Both rocks are mainly composed of fossils in a fine matrix: however, whereas the Purbeck stone features small snails, the rock at Frosterley is mainly composed of corals with fewer shells. The local quarrymen recognised two distinct varieties: 'cockle marble' and the finer 'pea marble'. The quality of the final rock is attributable to polishing, which can transform the detail of the coral features into delicate pale wisps or even starry cobwebs set in a darker matrix. Weathering quickly fades the polish, and the pristine dark-grey rock found in streams and quarries only bears a limited resemblance to the final product found in building interiors, although the corals are still clearly visible. A good exposure of the rock is available in the Bollihope Burn at the west end of Harehope Quarry, south of Frosterley, but there are a range of other sites in the dale where it also appears.

The primary advantage of the Frosterley quarries was that they could provide a high quality local source of ornamental rock that was ideal for use in prestigious buildings. For sites such as Durham, the rock could even be conveniently floated down the Wear on rafts. In Durham Cathedral, it is most abundant in the celebrated Chapel of the Nine Altars (despite some later restoration work). Other notable local sites include the Bishop's Palace in Bishop Auckland and in several churches, such as Frosterley, Stanhope, Brancepeth and Durham St. Mary-le-bow, but its renown is such that it has been exported and used worldwide (for example, Bombay Cathedral in India).

Bollihope valley from Hill End, with the 'Elephant Trees' on the skyline

As a result of this industry, many features of the original Bollihope landscape have gone, including most of the 'fairy hole' cave system that was also once used as an illegal gambling den. It might be thought that the scale of the workings would have left a dead sterile landscape, but the scenery at Bollihope has instead a peculiar attraction. The stream is typically lively and rushes through a gorge and fine woodlands, whilst the workings have left an unusual assemblage of conical mounds and vegetated cliffs. Nature is gradually reclaiming the terrain and creating a combination of man-made and natural surroundings that is a distinctive aspect of the Weardale scene. Indeed, the proximity to the public road and pleasant streamside haughs has meant that parts of the valley have become popular picnic sites on summer weekends.

Prominent in views from lower Weardale, especially around Frosterley or from the Bollihope valley, are a curious group of wind-sculptured beech trees on the southern skyline at Sunniside Edge. Locally, these features are known as the 'Elephant Trees', which may initially seem a fanciful comparison, but in certain numinous conditions a family of pachyderms linked trunk-to-tail can indeed be seen on the crest of the hill ....!

The main commercial centre of Weardale is at *Stanhope*, which has managed to retain some of its former aura of importance and prosperity. The parish church of St. Thomas has some parts dating from the 13th century, with shafts of the local 'Frosterley marble' incorporated in the interior. In the churchyard is the curio of the fossil tree, transplanted here from its original site of discovery on Edmundbyers Common.

Stanhope once had a bustling market (dating back to a charter granted in 1669) that prospered as the surrounding mining and quarrying industries expanded. This affluence is also reflected in the grandiose buildings now known as Stone Houses and the Old Rectory, both former rectory buildings. The extravagance of these church buildings reflected the wealth of the large Stanhope parish due to its tithe on the local mines and the avarice of some of the parsons then. However, later clergy were not quite so self-serving and one of the leading figures, Bishop Barrington, used part of the income to build and endow a series of schools throughout the dale.

On the west side of the town is Stanhope Hall, founded in the 13th century and later developed into one of the largest fortified houses in Weardale: comfort dictated major modifications in the 17th century but some early features have survived such as the mullioned and transomed windows. By contrast, the ornate crenulated hall of Stanhope Castle is a more recent edifice, being built in 1798 by the wealthy landowner and member-of-parliament Cuthbert Rippon, who owned at least 94 farms in the surrounding area.

The upper Bollihope valley

Fossil tree, Stanhope churchyard

The Butts area of Stanhope was once the sector used for archery practice, but has since been redefined by a series of elegant Georgian houses. With the decline of industry, agriculture has returned to its prime role in the local economy and the annual show in September continues to be an important event. The riverside promenade is a favourite walk for townsfolk and in summer the road ford with stepping stones across the Wear becomes a popular site. The depth of water at the ford can be rather deceptive, however, and there is a long history of motorists having to be rescued from their cars when the river becomes swollen by floodwater! In such conditions, the historic arched bridge located upstream at Briggen Winch gorge proves its worth: its age is undoubtedly very old, being widened in 1792 from an original structure which probably dates back to the 15th century.

The valley of Stanhope Burn was once a scene of major industrial activity. In addition to lead smelting at Stanhope Mill, the Weardale Iron Company established a blast furnace to produce steel, and higher up the valley was the site of the productive Stanhopeburn lead mine. There was also a series of extensive limestone quarries above this side-valley at West Pasture, with the lime processed in a row of kilns at Crawleyside. The same limestone band continues around the hillside from Crawleyside to produce the small caves at Linn Kirk above the Shittlehope Burn, but the famous Heatheryburn Caves (which provided a remarkable set of prehistoric finds including gold anklets that now reside in the British Musuem) no longer exist, having been removed by the quarrying at West Pasture.

In order to facilitate the growth of this industry, the remarkable *Stanhope & Tyne Railway* was built, and the old incline on the line can be seen adjacent to the B6278 road climbing up the steep hill from Crawleyside to Weatherhill. A little higher up the line are the old sandstone quarries at Parkhead, which gains its name from overlooking the top of the old deer forest of Waskerley Park. The remains of the park boundary palisade that was used to stockade the deer, known as the *Park Pale*, can still be traced as an embankment around and above the Waskerley Reservoir. Prominent landmarks in this vicinity are the communication masts on Collier Law, the summit of this fell marking the highest point (516m) of a broad sweep of moorland overlooking Stanhope.

One of the more remarkable aspects of the Stanhope & Tyne Railway, amongst its many distinctions, is that it actually reached Stanhope at a much earlier date (1834) than the valley railway following the obvious route up the dale. The reason for this was that the markets for the raw materials were to the north in the Tyne and Derwent valley. Although the valley railway had reached Wolsingham and Frosterley in 1847, it took until 1862 before it was extended to Stanhope.

Weardale and Stanhope from Hill End

Rookhope railway line on Bolt's Law

Stanhope & Tyne Railway

With the advent of the Industrial Revolution, the rich mineral resources of Weardale became increasingly lucrative, but exploitation was hindered by poor transport links. The steep-sided valley meant that the terrain was naturally unfavourable with roads often being in poor condition, limiting the supply of materials to market. However, to ambitious 19th century businessmen in the era of Stephenson and Brunel, such obstacles were engineering challenges waiting to be overcome. One of the greatest achievements of the time was to construct a railway line from Stanhope over the fells to the industrial heartland of the coalfield and the wharves of the Tyne. The original purpose of the line was mainly to transport limestone, but this subsequently expanded to include ironstone and lead, whilst the returning wagons brought coal for use in kilns, smelters or houses.

Considerable innovation was necessary to establish the line, including rope-hauled or self-acting inclines, with carts drawn by both horses and locomotives. The link to the Stanhope quarries was by two major inclines at Crawleyside and Weatherhill, each operated by stationary hauling engines, involving a vertical descent of over 220m. The route down to Consett was no easier, involving further inclines at Waskerley and a cradle-operated lift to cross the deep ravine of Hownes Gill; the ravine crossing became a bottleneck therefore it was eventually replaced by the spectacular viaduct that still exists today. The small collection of buildings at Waskerley village, high on the moors, was used for repairs and housed the railway workers; it can therefore claim to be the first railway village in the world.

Tragedy struck when the line opened in 1834: a cable broke at Weatherhill and three people were killed. Finances were also precarious, including large wayleave rents (fees for land access), and therefore the company had not been operating for long before it went 'bust' in 1841 with debts of £300,000. This affair almost bankrupted Robert Stephenson who had unwisely become a shareholder and was therefore pursued by creditors. The line was eventually taken over by the Stockton & Darlington Railway. Another incline was built down to the blast furnace at Stanhope Dene in 1845 with a link also made to the nearby lead mines at Stanhopeburn.

Rookhope & Middlehope Branch-Lines

Following the initial development of the Stanhope line, the Weardale Iron Company saw major advantages in also linking with other places where they had an interest. By 1847, they had built a branch from the original line to connect their mines at Rookhope with the blast furnaces of Tow Law. The Rookhope branch met the Stanhope line at Parkhead and crossed the high flanks of Bolt's Law at a summit of 509m to become the highest standard-gauge line ever built in this country. The connection to Rookhope was by the Boltsburn Incline, a vertical distance of 190m on a 1-in-12 slope. In best railway tradition, a station near the summit was named Blanchland Station despite this village being more than 5km away in the Derwent valley! However, a short branch was later built across the moor to serve the Derwent Mines above Blanchland.

In the 1850s, the Weardale Iron Company built a further major extension from Rookhope to its workings near Westgate. The line proceeded south to Smailsburn, then via incline to Northgate, and finally almost level around the fell to Scutter Hill above the Middlehope valley. The Northgate incline was worked from a water balance system, by varying the amount of water to achieve the correct weight to transport the wagons. Another 1-in-5 incline was subsequently constructed on Scutter Hill to transport ore from the main Wear valley up to the end of the line.

Wear Valley Railway

Despite being mooted for a long time, actual progress in building a railway up the Wear valley was very slow. The valley railway reached Stanhope in 1862 and was finally extended to Wearhead in 1895. WM Egglestone was a major advocate of the new line and had published a booklet on its potential benefits (see *Bibliography*). As inclines were built from the quarries and mines down to the new railway, it gradually drew the lifeblood from the older rail lines crossing the fells to the north.

Closure of the Lines

Limestone production from Heights Quarry ensured the Middlehope branch continued until the 1920s when an incline was built down to the valley bottom, and the line was closed soon after. The Rookhope line was finally closed in 1943 and the Crawleyside incline abandoned in 1951. However, activity at Parkhead Quarry meant the remainder of the line to Consett survived until 1968. Nowadays, the embankments and cuttings are the main relics, together with the ruined winding houses from where wagons were drawn up and down the inclines. The engine from the Weatherhill winding house is now in the National Railway Museum in York. Rowley station, which was on the line above Consett, has been relocated to the Beamish Museum. At Redgate Head, above the Boltsburn Incline, are the remains of railway-workers' buildings, a steam boiler and the engine house. The dismantled lines provide an excellent walking or cycling trail across the high moorland and have been adapted by Durham County Council into the 'Waskerley Way'.

The valley railway experienced its own decline as the mines closed. Passenger services ended in 1953 and the line beyond the Eastgate cement works up to Wearhead was closed and lifted in 1968. However, industry in the lower dale kept that section of line viable for freight transport. Now that industry has gone, the line faces a rather uncertain future, predicated upon the growth of tourism in the dale. Reinstated passenger trains running between Wolsingham and Stanhope have proved popular, and the prospect of re-establishing the downvalley link with Bishop Auckland remains an appealing possibility.

On the south side of the Wear at Stanhope, an incline from the valley railway provided a link with the large Newlandside Quarry. This site also marks the former location of the highly productive Cambokeels Mine and is one of the Weardale localities where multiple workings have developed at different stages, with excavations taking place both on the surface and deep below. The wooded course of the Horsley Burn is an archetypical contrast: an unspoilt stream falling to the valley in a series of pleasant cascades.

The village of *Eastgate* marks one of the original entrances to the bishopric's Stanhope Park. Built into a wall by the main road is a copy of the Roman altar found on this site, dedicated to Silvanus, god of huntsmen (the original is now at Durham University). Until 2005, the village was rather dominated by the large nearby cement works with its lofty chimney. The raw material for the works came from the massive limestone quarry on the southern hillside, with the connection being by a long conveyor tube. Now the site is another relic of the dale's industrial past with the derelict ground awaiting a new use. Although generally masked by trees, the quarry has removed a large area of hillside once known for its prehistoric relics. It has also unfortunately impinged on the Fairy Holes cave system above the Westernhope Burn (also known as the Kiddley Holes), which has one of the longest natural subterranean passages in the North Pennines. Cavers surveying these passages have given vivid names to some of them such as Coral Gallery, Sarcophagus and Grave Chamber: they also found inscriptions from the old miners who had also explored here in the past. The mischievous fairies from the caves were once said to be responsible for numerous pranks in the vicinity, such as curdling the milk or skimming-off the cream!

At Eastgate, the Rookhope Burn reaches the main valley in an attractive series of waterfalls that after heavy rain become an impressive spectacle. A bridge by the old corn mill provides a grandstand view of the horseshoe-shaped Low Linn and the upper plunge of High Linn, the latter sensitively restored together with a flume for water level monitoring. A little upstream, above another prominent fall, is the picturesque Turn Wheel, where a band of dark whinstone interrupts the smooth flow of water, forcing the stream into a whirl of rocks and water as it curves through a twisting chicane. The whinstone outcrop is a section of the Little Whin Sill, a thinner branch of the main 'sill' feature which is so prominent in Teesdale. Near to Stanhope, the same outcrop crosses the main valley and has been quarried in Greenfoot Quarry, near Briggen Winch.

The village of *Rookhope* nestles deep within the long side-valley of that name which branches off at Eastgate and contains extensive relics of lead and ironstone mining. Major mines were located in the immediate vicinity of the village at Boltsburn and Stotfield Burn, with the extensive 'flats' discovered at Boltsburn Mine making it one of the richest mines in the country during the early 20th century. The Blackett-Beaumont company had worked Boltsburn before this but it was only when the Weardale Lead Company took over the mine that the 'flats' were found, as they were separated from the main vein by a section of barren rock. Further up the Rookhope valley, mining has also occurred at Fulford, Rispey, Wolfcleugh and Groverake, whilst during the 1960s a new mine was opened at Redburn that discovered large quantities of fluorspar.

Rookhope, with the Boltsburn incline on the hill beyond

The conspicuous ruined arch over the burn just above Rookhope village is a remnant of the viaduct carrying the flue from the smelting complex at Lintzgarth Mill. The course of the flue can clearly be traced up the hillside to the remains of a distant chimney. Both lead-smelting hearths and a silver refinery operated in the mill, but difficult economic conditions caused closure in 1919. However, mining continued in the valley until quite recently because of the extensive fluorspar resources adjacent to the old lead workings. The shafthead winding gear from the fluorspar mine at Groverake (also known as Frazer's Grove) remains a prominent landmark in the upper Rookhope valley, and the spectacular fluorite crystals from Boltsburn Mine have found their way into museums around the world.

Turn Wheel, Rookhope Burn

The Moormaster & Mine Operators

Mining has taken place in Weardale since at least medieval times, and probably earlier as Roman coins have been found near Slitt Mine. In the 16th century, the Bishop of Durham created the post of Moormaster to oversee the management of the mines. This appointee was often a friend or relative and had substantial power over the granting of mining leases. Subsequently, the large mining operations of the Blackett-Beaumont family and London Lead Company became involved and the post of Moormaster could be leased from the bishopric, as well as the rights to work the numerous veins. Ironstone was also extracted by the Weardale Iron Company from extensive opencast workings at several sites.

After the main 'boom' had passed, smaller operators such as the Weardale Lead Company took over the more productive mines, eventually moving to fluorspar production in the 20th century for use in the steel industry. Fluorspar processing continued into the 1970s, but then began a rapid decline, with the last mine (Frazer's Grove) closing in 1999. Rather ironically, the only active mine nowadays is at Rogerley, which occasionally supplies rare specimens for mineral collectors.

Groverake (Frazer's Grove) Mine

The Rookhope Ryde

Rookhope stands in a pleasant place,
If the false thieves would let it be;
But away they steal our goods apace,
And ever an ill death may they dee.

In addition to its mining history, the name of Rookhope is widely-known for a famous skirmish that occurred in 1569. This happened during the 'Rising of the North', when most of the local men had been called away to help defend Barnard Castle against the pro-Catholic rebels. A raid by a group of Border Reivers took six hundred sheep and other livestock, but the alarm was raised and the raiders were intercepted by a local posse on Nookton Fell (near Hunstanworth). During the resulting combat, four of the Reivers were killed and eleven captured at the cost of one local man. Such encounters between raiders and local defenders were not uncommon but this particular event has lived on because the details were then celebrated through a lyrical 24-verse ballad known as 'The Rookhope Ryde'.

The upper Rookhope valley was also extensively worked for ironstone, with the hillsides clearly modified by the opencasting. A rail line was constructed to link the iron workings and lead mines in the upper valley with the Boltsburn incline. Higher up, at the head of the valley, the road crosses over into Allendale by the desolate pass of Shorngate crowned by a fine currick at its summit.

Returning to the main Wear valley, the route from Eastgate to Westgate is through the territory of Stanhope Park, where any settlement was originally excluded by the Bishop of Durham. Pressure for land eventually led to permission for limited development within the park boundaries in the 15th century and a few new farms were built. The minor road south of the river passes Westburnhope, Ludwell and Swinhopeburn, each dating from this time and retaining interesting vernacular features. On the north side of the dale, the landscape of the park has been considerably altered by quarrying on the slopes of Cuthbert's Heights. At the opposite end of the old Park, *Westgate* forms an attractive twin village to Eastgate, but there are only scant remains of its old castle. The little group of houses at the adjacent hamlet of Weeds marks one of the original shielings developed just outside the boundary of the park. To the south, the Swinhope Burn tumbles down to the main valley by a series of stepped waterfalls partly hidden in the trees. This is the same stream that higher up drains a large area of fell often holding late snow, hence the ski-tow of the Weardale Ski Club at Swinhopehead.

Amongst the most sublime attractions in the dale is the deep gorge of the Middlehope Burn. To enter it, a beckoning path from old Westgate corn mill leads alongside foaming waterfalls into the enchanted realm of *Slitt Wood*. Sheltered by the beautiful woodlands and limestone scarps of the gorge is a rewardingly rich and diverse flora. Their presence seems all the more remarkable when considering the scale of mineral working revealed 1km into the valley at Slitt Mine. The mine relics also have much of interest including the bousesteems used to store ore next to the dressing floor, and the pits for the water-wheels used to provide crushing power. A curious flat-arched double bridge has been constructed over the burn to optimise space on the narrow valley floor. Higher up the valley is Middlehope Mine which has further extensive remains, including the gated entrance to the important horse-level originally driven by the London Lead Company in 1806. Subsequently, ownership of this mine passed to the Blackett-Beaumonts and then the Weardale Iron Company, with the latter using the main level to excavate substantial ironstone 'flats' next to the lead veins. During the month of May, the old workings in the valley become delicately spangled with the tiny white flowers of spring sandwort and the showy petals of the mountain pansy.

Ironstone was also extensively worked at nearby Slitt Pasture and exported by the Weardale Iron Company's railway over the fell to Rookhope. At its peak during the 1870s, 30,000 tons of ore was being transported each year. These ironstone workings have left an interesting relic at West Rigg Opencut on Scutter Hill, where opencasting of the iron 'flats' exposed and left behind the lead vein from which the 'flats' were originally formed. In the centre of the vein is a slit-like gash (the 'oreshoot') where the lead ore was removed long before the ironstone was worked, presumably by the 'Old Man': the parts of the vein now remaining are waste pillars on either side of the ore. West Rigg therefore provides an unusually clear view of the relationship between a lead vein and its adjacent rocks.

The next settlement to be reached is Daddry Shield, consisting of further rows of cottages built for miners and farm workers. The main road then arrives at *St. John's Chapel*, centred upon its grouping of church, hall and shops around the village green. Originally the site had a chapel-at-ease to be used by the Bishop of Durham whilst on hunting visits but this was replaced by the 18th century church. Morley Egglestone affectionately described St. John's Chapel as the 'metropolis' of the upper dale on account of its auction mart and annual fair. Those days have gone, but every year, when the agricultural show arrives in late August, some of the bustle of the past does return. A minor road to Upper Teesdale departs from the village to cross the fells at Harthope Head (609m) with the upper slopes culminating in Chapelfell Top (703m). The lower slopes generally have more of interest, notably the lovely waterfalls of the Harthope Burn or the caves and rock-gorge at Clints Crags in the adjacent Ireshope valley.

Westburnhope

Middlehope Burn and the old bouseteems at Slitt Mine

Limestone gorge, Clints Crags

Ireshopeburn village has a particularly interesting Methodist chapel which dates back to 1760 and was the first of its type to be built in the valley; the adjacent manse now houses an excellent museum of local history. The chapel with its archetypal simplicity and informal tiered interior is believed to be the second oldest chapel in continuous use (after Newbiggin in Teesdale). At New House, on the north side of the valley, the cluster of buildings is centred on the grand country house built by William Blackett as the centre of his company's mining operations in the dale. Miners would gather here once a year for 'the Pays', together with other trades such as millers, doctors and grocers, who had wooden huts from which to then settle their accounts with the miners; travelling salesmen such as Hexham hatters and Yorkshire blanket-makers would also attend to promote their wares and do business.

The Blackett-Beaumont company also provided the funds, together with contributions from the miners themselves, to build the local school, now the Weardale Inn. One of the company mines was at Blackdene, where exploration had taken place since medieval times; after lead became uneconomic it was converted into a fluorspar mine and operated until the 1980s under the auspices of British Steel. A particularly attractive section of the river occurs nearby at West Blackdene, where the waters fall over stepped shelves below the arched bridge, overlooked by a charmingly-restored row of old miners' houses.

Intake pastures, Daddry Shield

Drystone Walls and Enclosure Land

The Enclosure Acts of the 17th to 19th centuries created a large demand for stone walls to demarcate boundaries. Land was also parcelled into individual fields to control stock grazing, also traditionally defined by walls (today fences are more common) and often with a stone barn. Even higher parts of the fell were occasionally over-optimistically enclosed as 'allotments' to try and bring them into cultivation. The effect of this agricultural compartmentalisation is particularly well displayed in upper Weardale, where the walls produce intricate geometric patterns dividing the valley pastures into a patchwork of different fields. Occasional enclosure 'roads' interrupt the pattern, linking the valley floor with the upper fell to provide access to the higher land. However, by contrast with other areas, field barns ('laithes') to store hay are less common.

Building the walls was, and still is, a skilled craft with the stones carefully positioned to maximise structural integrity, usually by a double-wall with through-stones. Despite their longevity, and some have clearly been present for centuries, walls do occasionally 'rush' under pressure from stock or weather. 'Wallers' therefore continue to be required to conduct occasional repairs.

Methodism and John Wesley

The role of Methodism amongst the isolated communities of the North Pennines has been substantial, particularly in Weardale (and also the Allendales). As the influence of the Bishops of Durham declined in the dale, so the disaffection of common people with the clergy grew, and they became increasingly open to alternatives.

Particular resentment was created by the avarice of the Church, which was able to extract huge levies from the mining industry. In addition to the Bishop's Lot, which was a ninth portion of the mined ore, there was also a tithe of one tenth which was due to the local parson. As a result of this, the clergy became rather wealthy, and for a while Stanhope was even reputed to be the richest parish in England (in 1832, the annual income was close to £5000). However, the high rewards tended to attract social climbing personalities, who had less of an interest in the everyday needs of their parishioners: in the 19th century, three local parsons eventually reached the status of bishop. Money was also sometimes diverted into grandiose projects, such as the rectory buildings at Stanhope.

This wealth was apparently not enough for one of the parsons: records show that he even attempted to also exact a tithe on the Bishop's Lot! The latter dispute was apparently stimulated by the growth in Acts of Enclosure, which removed common land from the ordinary people and became another source of resentment against the 'high and mighty'.

For a time, Presbyterianism was strong in the dale, apparently introduced by an influx of settlers from north of the Border, with a church of that branch being established at Ireshopeburn. In the 18th century, word began to spread of the teachings of John Wesley, with the first Methodist mission to the dale being by Christopher Hopper in 1748, who travelled over the fells from Allendale to record a rather ambivalent welcome:

'It was a day storm of snow that we crossed the quagmires and enormous mountains into the dales, and we met with a cold reception. The enemy barricaded the place and made his bulwarks strong, but the Lord opened the heart of a poor Scotch shepherd….. The next day I preached under the walls of an old castle [Westgate castle]'

Despite these initial difficulties, Methodism soon established itself and stimulated by the influence of John Wesley, who first visited the dale in 1750, became the dominant religion. Numerous chapels were built throughout Weardale, as elsewhere in the North Pennines. The energetic Wesley visited the area several times, sometimes preaching at Weardale in the morning, Teesdale in the afternoon and Swaledale in the evening. His thirteenth and last visit was in 1790 when he was aged 87.

High House Chapel, Ireshopeburn

At Wearhead village, site of the former rail terminus, Burnhope Burn and Killhope Burn meet to form the River Wear. In the valley of the former stream, *Burnhope Reservoir* was completed in 1937 to provide water for Consett and Wearside, and now provides one of the more popular sites in the upper dale. Its construction resulted in the abandonment of six farms and the small hamlet of Burnhope Toun, a place-name indicative of the Scottish influence hereabouts.

A little further up the main valley are the attractive settlements at *Cowshill* and *Burtreeford*, clustered together around the junction of Killhope Burn and Sedling Burn. Both streams have attractive waterfalls, with the Killhope Burn leaping over an abrupt rocky step to form the ebullient cascade of Burtree Linn. Here is another tranquil locale which was formerly a hive of industry. The valley of Sedling Burn has a profusion of old mine workings with Burtree Pasture Mine and Sedling Mine being two of the most productive in Weardale; after being extensively worked for lead through the centuries, Burtree Pasture went into fluorspar extraction and only closed as recently as 1981. The mine-levels continue underground to link with those at Groverake Mine in the Rookhope valley. Just above Cowshill are the old Queensbury ironstone workings, and upstream from Burtree Linn is a quarry, now flooded by a sinister pool, where an outcrop of whinstone was exploited. The quarry is well-known geologically because it displays the faultline of the Burtreeford Disturbance, abruptly tilting down the rocks on its eastern side.

Above Cowshill, the main valley begins to become more enclosed and austere. At Killhopeburn Bridge, the Wellhope Burn joins from a remote upland valley. The main road continues by the Killhope Burn with the valley pastures soon diminishing to be replaced by conifer plantations and moorland heather.

Set amidst these normally bleak surroundings are the remains of Killhopehead Mine, another highly productive mine of its time, now imaginatively converted into the *Killhope Lead Mining Centre*. Major lead veins intersect with the stream bed here and were therefore exploited for many centuries, with a series of old 'hushes' hidden in the trees near to the mine. When the Blackett-Beaumont company took up the lease, they systematically drove the Park Level to provide access to all of the veins at the head of the valley, most of which were found to contain good lodes of ore. Water power for the large crushing mill and for dressing the ore was provided by an extensive system of leats and later two dams were built on the hillside above.

The Killhope site has now been extensively developed by Durham County Council as an interpretative centre and museum for the lead-mining industry. Large water-wheels have been restored both on the surface and underground in a re-opened part of the Park Level. The largest wheel (the 'Killhope Wheel') is over 10m in diameter and was built by the famous engineering company of WG Armstrong: it was originally installed at Holmes Linn in East Allendale but later transferred to this mine. Most commendably, the infrastructure of both the crushing mill and the dressing floor has also been reconstructed, together with the bousesteems and a simulation of the horrors of the mine lodging 'shop'. This provides an excellent insight into the hard physical labour and harsh conditions experienced by the miners and their families.

Also visible from the Killhope mine museum are the buildings and small enclosures on the north side of the valley that formed miner's smallholdings at an altitude in excess of 500m. In 1871, over 1000 people are recorded as living in upper Weardale west of Cowshill and as a result many lived in such marginal situations: now, they are less than 100 people here. The old track of the Carriers' Way snakes up this hill, providing the route by which ore was transported by packhorses over to Allenheads for smelting. Meanwhile, the A689 road continues to climb upwards beyond the mine buildings, and the fells finally close in on the valley floor.

A final steep ascent leads to the road summit at *Killhope Cross*, its elevation of 627m above sea-level making it the highest road pass in England. The cross itself is easily passed unnoticed but sits unobtrusively by the roadside marking the boundary between County Durham and Cumbria. All around is a vast expanse of peat, heather, tussock grass and bog.

Upper Weardale at Burtreeford

Killhope Wheel and mine centre

Harthope Burn

Hexhamshire Common

Derwentdale and Devil's Water

The scenes which, all enchanting, threw their spell
O'er old King Arthur, who in dreamy state,
Abides for ever caverned in this dell;

The Derwent Valley, Alexander Barrass

This north-eastern corner of the Pennines contains the well-known upper reaches of the River Derwent and the much less frequented valley of the Devil's Water. Both are surrounded by rolling moors, and have a distinctive natural charm enhanced by a series of attractive villages. The northern limits are clearly demarcated by the populous Tyne valley with historic Hexham as the main settlement. To the east, the upland fringe is bounded by a marked transition into the more industrial landscape of the coalfield with the old steel town of Consett prominent: the A68 road provides a convenient boundary here. The River Derwent has historically been the border between the County Palatine of Durham and the autonomous liberty of Hexhamshire, with much of this chapter territorially in the land of the old Regality.

The Derwent is named from the Celtic word 'derw' meaning oak tree and there are several rivers of that name in the country. It is particularly appropriate for the Derwent of the North Pennines: in times past, its valley was renowned for the quality of its oakwoods. Nowadays, the main association is probably with the large *Derwent Reservoir*, which flooded a large area of valley in the 1960s. Sympathetic landscaping means that the reservoir blends in subtly with the surrounding landscape and, from most viewpoints, the grass-covered embankment of the dam merges inconspicuously with the nearby pastures. Yachts skim playfully across the lake on breezy days and its banks have pleasant picnic sites, whilst the western end has become a favoured site for roosting water-birds.

Edmundbyers is a handsome village situated at a meeting of the ways near the reservoir dam. The village is old, with Anglo-Saxon origins, and the extensively-restored church of St. Edmund's retains original Norman elements in the nave and chancel. To the south, lead mines in the Burnhope valley were developed on a relatively small scale, with the most prominent ruins now being that of Feldon smelt mill with its conspicuous hillside flue. The same valley is now characterised by a series of deserted and derelict farmsteads: Pedam's Oak reputedly gaining its unusual name from an outlaw who once regularly hid in a hollow tree there. The economics of hill-farming have waxed and waned over time, and the marginal land around these exposed farms required continual effort to keep it viable. As with many upland communities, the loss of youth and vitality during the 20th century proved to be the critical threshold from which there was no return.

The Regality of Hexhamshire

Hey for the buff and the blue,
Hey for the cap and the feather,
Hey for the bonny lass true,
That lives in Hexhamshire

The history of the Regality dates back to 674AD when the Archbishop of York assumed control of a district stretching from the Derwent valley to South Tynedale, including the Allendales. For much of the Middle Ages, the archbishops therefore administered the wider territory of the Shire from Hexham as an autonomous liberty. However, the relationship with York was summarily ended at the time of the Reformation and Henry VIII appropriated the district for the crown.

Subsequently, the estates of Hexhamshire were transferred through a series of land purchases, and eventually much of it came into the possession of the wealthy Blackett family, who became even more prosperous as they exploited its mineral riches. Meanwhile the administrative functions of the old Regality became incorporated into the county of Northumberland. The 'liberty' of the district now rests with much of it being a quiet rural retreat with an air of seclusion and tranquillity. In particular, the vast open spaces of Hexhamshire Common provide a broad landscape of sweeping moorland and big skies, enlivened in late summer by the vivid bloom of heather and the sweet bilberries found on its rocky outcrops.

Derwent Reservoir

Muggleswick and the Mosstroopers

The isolated position of Muggleswick made it a favoured raiding target for the notorious Border mosstroopers. On one particular occasion in 1528 a raid led by Willie o' Shotlyngton, from the Bellingham district of Northumberland, was subsequently pursued by the local militia. The raiders were unable to escape across the Tyne, due to flooding and barred bridges, and therefore vengeance was swift: most of the raiders were either killed, or captured and swiftly executed.

Despite this history of bloody conflict, local records indicate that the mosstroopers' familiarity with Muggleswick subsequently led to some of them settling in the vicinity! The rich pickings of nearby Weardale and Teesdale would have been an undoubted lure. One of the more infamous figures was Rowley Harrison who lived at The Shield and died in 1712: although now having a grave in Muggleswick churchyard, he was originally buried outside its boundaries. Another disreputable character from this time, Thomas Raw of Wharnley Burn (near Allensford), was also refused consecrated ground in many of the local parishes. After his death in 1715, he was therefore buried on the crest of the hill behind his house, a slab gravestone afterwards being placed over the burial site.

Below the Derwent Reservoir, and prominent on a ridge above the river valley, is the small hamlet of *Muggleswick*. Amongst the group of buildings are the impressive ruins of the Grange, formerly a three-storey medieval building with a large hall above the basement (photo: p.111). The gable end also contains a large blocked three-light window, suggesting that it lit an upper living room (or *solar*) above the main hall. The Grange was constructed about 1260 by Prior Hugh de Darlington from the priory of Durham, and acted as a base for managing the adjacent Muggleswick Park: a forge was used to produce local ironwork. The unenclosed upper slopes of the park remain a feature of the landscape today, covered with bracken and heather, and criss-crossed by paths that provide sumptuous open views of the Derwent valley and surrounding moors.

During the 17th century, the Muggleswick district became a place of religious dissent. At the time of Cromwell's Commonwealth, a puritanical Presbyterianism became established in the parish and then resisted the return of religious orthodoxy on the Restoration of the monarchy. When the authorities were mistakenly informed that Catholics were involved in this resistance, they felt compelled to act, with twelve local men being arrested and jailed. The affair became known as the Muggleswick Park Conspiracy, but after a detailed inquiry discovered little evidence beyond a general disenchantment with the Church, the arrested men were released. In the churchyard at Muggleswick is also reputedly interred an infamous local giant called Edward Ward: no records remain of his burial but, for whatever reason, there are frequent references to giants in the rich folklore of the Derwent valley.

Near Muggleswick, the river Derwent snakes a sinuous course through a deep twisting gorge. Tributary streams have carved their own twisting courses towards the river, producing a complex topography of narrow ridges and deep valleys. This is a hidden land of steep intricate slopes, luxuriantly wooded with lichen-encrusted trees that are often gnarled and hoary, reaching back deep into history. In spring and summer, the sheltered location also encourages a remarkably varied and colourful flora. One of the river bends has incised a horseshoe-shaped loop around a steep elevated nose of land known as *The Sneep* (or The Snape). Another loop is known as Silver Tongue from the old mine that was formerly delved into its banks, the dwelling here still being known as Lead Mill Cottage. The beautiful wooded dells containing Hisehope Burn and Horsleyhope Burn also provide a series of hidden delights, with a narrow road negotiating the ravine at Comb Bridges by a suite of steep hairpins. The slopes to the east of Horsleyhope contain the remnants of the Healeyfield Lead Mine and smelt mill, located within another interesting wooded dell at Dene Howl. As at Silvertongue, this mine was renowned for a high silver content that once supplied the Bishop of Durham's mint.

> **The Sneep and the Legend of King Arthur**
>
> *King Arthur's round table is near,*
> *Though none has declared how it came,*
> *He lifts up his head once a year,*
> *The sceptre long lost to reclaim,*
> *Enchantment its hold must forego,*
> *Could any strange arm draw the sword,*
> *The trumpet could any man blow,*
> *That lie at the feet of their lord.*
>
> The Derwent: An Ode
John Carr (18th century)
>
> The deep snaking gorge of The Sneep has an intriguing link with the myths of King Arthur. Legend tells of a cave below the promontory that is inaccessible to mere mortals, in which the mythical king is sleeping together with Queen Guinevere and several knights. This would certainly concur with general Arthurian lore: after the king was mortally wounded in battle with his arch-enemy Mordred, his body was then described as having been spirited away by fairies to have the wounds healed. Then the fairy folk placed King Arthur in a deep sleep and concealed him in a cave hidden by dense foliage awaiting a future call-to-arms.
>
> To break the king's enchantment, someone must successfully find and enter the cave. Once inside the hidden grotto, the would-be liberator must be able to lift the sword of Excalibur, then cut a garter and blow a bugle waiting on a nearby table. If the quest is triumphant, the king and his knights will be roused into action again.
>
> Of course, there are many other sites in Britain that have an Arthurian association, some that even mention a cave too! Nevertheless, a grave barrow and cremation pot have been found near The Sneep giving a historic foundation to the local legend, and suggesting that something extraordinary happened here a long time ago.
>
> The Sneep certainly represents an appropriate site for the legend: the density of the woodlands and the broken, craggy slopes on which they flourish mean that it would be highly unlikely that the king's peaceful slumber would be broken. The trees are relicts of the ancient oakwood that was once much more extensive throughout the region and this sanctuary for plants and animals is now a designated nature reserve. Survival of the woodlands can mainly be attributed to the inaccessibility of the precipitous slopes within the deep gorge, but is all the more remarkable considering the development of nearby industry, including the Healeyfield, Hysop and Silvertongue lead mines.

The Derwent valley near Silvertongue and The Sneep

In addition to Muggleswick and The Sneep, other place-names hereabouts are quite distinctive, adding to the rich store of lore and legend in the Derwent valley: Crooked Oak takes its unusual name from a prominent tree in the bend of the river, whilst Wallish Walls is apparently from 'Welsh Walls' as the Anglo-Saxons would refer to any of the native Celtic peoples as being Welsh. By contrast, the influence of the Church is manifest in the naming of Minsteracres, linking with the archbishopric of York, and by Durham Field, which is an historic property of the Bishop of Durham located just over the county boundary within the territory of Northumberland.

In the past, the old farmhouse at Crooked Oak had a particular reputation as a place of witchcraft. One of its inhabitants, Jane Frizzle, was reputed to flit about the Derwent valley on her favourite broomstick. The entire district, in fact, was rather notorious as a favourite rendezvous for witches.

In 1673 a hearing at Morpeth sessions heard several witnesses describe various 'black arts' being enacted amongst the villages and farms of the area. These actions were said to include the bewitching of farm animals and tales of named individuals transforming themselves into cats. In addition, lurid stories were told of people being placed under a witch's spell then fitted with a bridle and ridden like a horse!

... I came at last to Blanchland. And Blanchland more than any other village I saw, deserves special mention. My walk along the valley had prepared me to expect rather a pretty place of flowery gardens and rose-covered cottages, and my map had told me that there was a church with a tower. And all these there are, but it is not these that make Blanchland spring vividly to mind when long after, you live again your travels in retrospect.

Alfred Wainwright 1938[1]

Above the Derwent Reservoir, *Blanchland* is the main settlement in the valley, set in a secluded location by the river. The beautiful setting certainly enhances the scene, but the unique character of the village is essentially a legacy of its rich monastic history.

The White Monks of the Premonstratensian Order first established an abbey here in 1165 and so gave the village its name after the colour of their habits. The prominent gatehouse (which now serves as the village post office) was the formal entrance into the abbey precinct from the north and was also used to house the poorer travellers passing through the village, in a large communal room. Through the gate, one enters a large courtyard enclosed by rows of cottages that acted as dormitory and refectory for the monks, or as estate offices and workshops. Within this setting, the monks would both go about their daily rituals of worship in the abbey church and also spend time managing their various sources of income coming from the land owned by the order.

The scourge of the Border raiders remained a constant threat to the abbey. On one such raid, the brigands had missed the village to become lost in the mist on Dead Friar's Fell further south. Unfortunately, when the monks then rang the abbey bells to acclaim their salvation, the raiders were alerted to the location of the village and managed to re-direct their mission of plunder and slaughter. After the dissolution of the monasteries by Henry VIII, the lands were confiscated by the Crown and the abbey itself became a manor house.

Continuing depravations by raiders and local foraging of the stone for building materials resulted in the village falling into disuse and disrepair. By the time of John Wesley's visit in 1747, he regretfully described it in his journal as 'little more than a heap of ruins'. The land around Blanchland had meanwhile passed to the Forster family and then Lord Crewe, Bishop of Durham (1674-1721). As the bishop died without an heir, his estates became incorporated within the Lord Crewe Charitable Trust and, as part of this large bequest, the restoration of Blanchland was begun.

Most of what we see in the village today is from this 18th century rebuilding work. Particularly well restored is the beautiful abbey church, integrating the 14th century tower and chancel. The abbot's lodging, the guesthouse and the kitchen have now been incorporated into the inn of the Lord Crewe Arms, which also features a magisterial portrait of the Bishop with his influential wife, Dorothy Forster. At the back of the inn is a lawn containing the remains of both the abbey cloisters and the Chapter House.

Blanchland is especially charming at dusk on a tranquil evening, when the daily visitors have gone on their way. Twilight lengthens the shadows and accentuates the peculiar ambience of the village allowing the imagination more freedom in recreating the medieval scene. At any time of day, ample distraction is provided by the fine valley woodlands and pleasant river scenery.

In times past, however, this quiet backwater at the head of the Derwent valley was once considerably more active. It acted as the hub for a network of historic trading routes that radiate across the moors to adjacent valleys and also provided a focal point for cattle drovers travelling southwards to market. The village was also the centre for a small but intensive mining industry that developed in the surrounding hills.

---

[1] *From 'A Pennine Journey' by A. Wainwright published by Frances Lincoln Ltd, copyright © The Estate of A. Wainwright, 1986, 2004. Reproduced by permission of Frances Lincoln Ltd.*

Restored cottages

The gatehouse

Abbey church

Outside the monastic precinct

Pumping station, Ramshaw

Hunstanworth

The Derwent Mines

The derelict lead-smelting mill,
Flued to its chimney up the hill,
That smokes no answer any more
But points, a landmark on Bolt's Law,
The finger of all questions.
New Year Letter, W H Auden, 1940

To the south of Blanchland, Boltshope valley has long been renowned for its rich mineral lodes. Together with other workings in the vicinity, notably at Shildon Mine, but also at Beldon Shields and Reeding, these have historically been called the Derwent Mines. The main series of workings in the Boltshope valley are located around the scattering of houses at Ramshaw. Here are the remains of Jeffrey's Mine and Ramshaw Mine, with Whiteheaps Mine a little further south.

The prominent building located just off the Stanhope road is the pumping house established on the site of the Presser Engine Shaft (Jeffrey's Mine) in 1906 by the Consett Water Company: it is now used by Northumbria Water for a contingency water supply. Jeffrey's Mine had a smelt mill and the flues can be traced up the hill to terminate at the conspicuous chimney high on the moor next to Sikehead Dam. The other chimney here, just to the west, marks the later Sikehead (or East Whiteheaps) Mine, which had a small steam winch installed over the shaft in the 20th century; the remains of the wheel pits and an engine house are also still visible. A third chimney used to also stand on the eastern side of the Stanhope road at Taylor's Shaft but was struck by lightning and collapsed in 1974. Unlike the other mines, Whiteheaps operated until quite recently, supplying fluorspar for the steel industry, but closed in 1989.

During the 18th century, operations were directed by the London Lead Company, but after a dispute with the landowner, the lease eventually passed to the Derwent Mining Company. The workings became extensive, employing over 250 men underground by the 1860s, with long shafts over 100 fathoms deep (ca. 200m). Steam engines had been installed to replace water power, but when a reliable system of water flow was developed, the waterwheels were reinstated as the power supply was much cheaper. Water came from reservoirs on the moor, augmented by a series of leats cut across the hillside to intercept drainage from a wider catchment. Most of the storage was provided by the Sikehead Dam reservoir, with the water driving hydraulic pressure engines and water wheels at each of the mines. After the Weardale Iron Company built its Rookhope railway, a branch was extended to Sikehead in the 1860s and inclines from the mines ran up to this line. This also allowed a better supply of coal facilitating the use of steam engines again to pump the deep shafts.

Sikehead Mine and Jeffrey's Mill chimney

Riddlehamhope

On Dead Friar's Fell, looking to Sandyford

The River Derwent begins where Nookton Burn and Beldon Burn meet at the Gibraltar Rock to the west of Blanchland. One of the old ways over the moors follows the valley of the Beldon Burn to Riddlehamhope on the flanks of Newbiggin Fell. Although now only a sad ruin, Riddlehamhope is a large distinctive house often described as being a *bastle* (fortified farmhouse). Other decorative flourishes, such as the tall chimneys, suggest the defensive function was then modified at a later stage. Particularly notable is the clustering of its many windows on the south side, taking full advantage of the sunny aspect and open vista. The upland setting can be very attractive, especially in late summer with the heather in bloom.

South of Blanchland, the road to Stanhope passes above the Derwent Mines onto Dead Friar's Fell. The name of the fell commemorates an unfortunate member of the monk's brethren who lost his way at this remote site and perished in a blizzard. During a later storm, another stormbound traveller attempted to shelter by the inviting warmth of the nearby smelt mill flue, but was lethally overcome by the poisonous fumes. These fells often receive quite heavy snowfalls, with the weather station at nearby Boltshope Park often featuring in weather synopses because of its noteworthy snow-depths. The highest summit in the vicinity is Bolt's Law (540m), topped by a currick and triangulation pillar, with the prospect featuring a vast sweeping landscape of rolling heather moor stretching in all directions.

Overlooking the sylvan reaches of upper Derwentdale is the small village of *Hunstanworth*, positioned together with nearby Townfield. The unusual buildings here were designed by Samuel Teulon in 1862 to provide improved housing for workers at the Derwent Mines. Teulon has been bluntly described by Nikolaus Pevsner, in his descriptive guide to British buildings, as 'one of the more ruthless and assertive of the High Victorian rogue-architects'. However, Hunstanworth shows off quite well his particular interest for the Burgundian style of architecture, with an emphasis on patterned roof-tiles exemplified by the ornate church. The churchyard also has the remains of an old pele tower, a relic of the old settlement existing on this site and its need for defence from the Border raiders on account of the prominent elevated position. The heyday of the mines brought an influx of Cornish and Welsh workers into the village and surrounding area, leading to occasional conflict with local people: during one notorious event, police had to intervene to disperse a riotous situation at the old Miner's Arms in Baybridge. The population of Hunstanworth peaked at 778 people in 1861 and has rapidly declined since then.

Another historic track to the north of Blanchland passes the old engine house of Shildon Mine, which dates back to the 15th century and was amongst the first to install one of the new-fangled Cornish steam engines to pump out surplus water. The track then leads to the large isolated building and former inn at Pennypie House, a favourite halt for drovers following the traditional route across the moors from Hexham, which also had a smithy for shoeing cattle. The speciality of the inn was, as advertised, to provide a pie for a penny. For a hungry traveller tramping across the moors, this would have undoubtedly been a suitable enticement!

The Drove Ways

And over the highways and byeways I plod,
My clothes are all tattered, my feet are ill-shod,
But there isn't a roadway that I haven't trod,
Being forty-five summers a drover.
Life of a Drover, Packie Manus Byrne

One of the main cattle drovers' routes south from Scotland was across the moors from Hexham to Blanchland, proceeding then to Weardale and Teesdale on the way to large markets such as at Thirsk. The drovers would use high tracks over the moors to avoid conflicts on enclosed or cultivated land, and therefore many of their routes remain today. Typically, the drover would be in charge of 100-120 cattle, moving them down from the Highlands at a steady pace, and stopping at traditional safe 'stances' overnight for shelter and sustenance.

Also using the routes would be the usual eclectic mix of travellers living life 'on the road', including carriers, tinkers, badgers and pedlars with their assorted wares, and vagabonds excluded or expelled from normal society. The Longman's Grave near Pennypie House indicates the toll which the harsh life and ever-present risk of disease exacted upon these perpetual travellers.

To the north of the Derwent valley is the broad upland basin of the Devil's Water, with the main stream and its several tributaries draining the extensive moors of Hexhamshire Common. This has always been a relatively quiet district of rolling hillsides etched by deeply-cut stream valleys that shelter attractive woodlands. The many fine old farmhouses testify that farming has long been the mainstay of the local economy. More recently, a large section of the moors has been converted into the conifer plantations of Slaley Forest. Trials for lead mining did take place in the area, and there are 'Old Man' workings near Burntshieldhaugh, but little of any real significance was found. However, smelt mills were constructed at Blackhall and then at Dukesfield (by the Blackett-Beaumont company) to process Allendale lead ore: Dukesfield mill closed in the 1830s, but has parts of the arches and chimney remaining.

Old drove road at Pennypie House

The upper Devil's Water from Blanchland Common

Rolling mist on Hexhamshire Common, near Westburnhope

Having no major scenic highlights, the area around the Devil's Water is easily bypassed for more obvious destinations. However, as with much of the less well-known North Pennines, the landscape here is more of a subtle infusion rather than a heady mix, gradually insinuating its qualities rather than being dramatically revealing. Habitations are dispersed without having a particular nucleus, and there is a labyrinth of lanes eventually leading to cul-de-sacs towards the head of the valley. If a focal point needed to be nominated, then Whitley Chapel would be the obvious candidate due to its location at the convergence of the Devil's Water and Rowley Burn, and because it contains the handsome chapel of St. Helen's.

Various old routes from East Allendale cross Hexhamshire Common to reach the Devil's Water, including the Carriers' Way and the Broad Way. These were used both to transport lead ore to the mills and the finished lead casts ('pigs') to market. Other travellers would also have followed these upland tracks and the naming of nearby Hangman Hill presumably marks the site where thieves and other villains received summary justice.

The main route to Hexham from Slaley (B6306 road) passes Dipton Wood to cross the Devil's Water by the graceful span of Linnels Bridge. Downstream of the bridge, the river continues in fine woodlands to flow below the ruins of Dilston Castle, residence of the ill-fated last Earl of Derwentwater. When the earl supported the Old Pretender during the unsuccessful 1715 Jacobite rebellion, his estate became forfeit to the crown and he lost his head. The extensive estate included parts of Allendale and Alston Moor with their rich mineral resources.

The north-eastern Pennines end at the Tyne valley, where the large town of *Hexham* is the main attraction. Amongst the many historic market towns of northern England, Hexham inevitably ranks very highly on account of its proud heritage and handsome buildings.

The famous Abbey was built by Augustinian canons during the 12th and 13th century on the site of the 7th century St. Wilfred's church; the crypt is the only surviving feature of the original church which was built using stone partly taken from the Roman fort at Corbridge *(Corstopitum)*. Fortunately, extensive remains of the monastic influence exist both in and around the Abbey. Of particular interest is the night stair with its well-worn steps, which allowed monks direct access to the church from the dormitory. The nave is a much newer feature, being rebuilt in the early 20th century as the original structure was destroyed by the Scots. Nearby is the restored Moot Hall, which was formerly a 15th century gatehouse guarding a walled enclosure containing the prominent tower (the Old Gaol) that is now a heritage centre. Both these buildings were used by the archbishops of York from which to administer their Hexhamshire estates.

Linnels Bridge

Hexham Abbey

The monastic community and large bishopric meant that Hexham steadily grew to become an important market centre, trading goods from the surrounding farms, forests and mines. Its four guilds were Weavers, Hatters, Tanners and Shoemakers, and Skinners and Glovers: traders from these guilds would have strong links with the large rural hinterland that supplied raw materials and often purchased the finished goods. This prosperity is reflected in the many fine buildings in the town, notably on Market Street, Gilesgate, Fore Street and Battle Hill. In addition, an interesting 17th century town-house with impressive gables and mullioned windows has survived in the odd little street of Holy Island.

The archetypical view of Hexham is from the old nine-arched bridge over the Tyne, but a broader perspective may be gained from the ridge to the south on which the Racecourse is situated. The elevated setting and ample panorama over the North Pennines mean the Racecourse has one of the country's most attractive outlooks from such a venue. A little further south is the enchanting domain of West Dipton Woods, where the burn has carved a remarkably deep gorge through attractive woodland above Dipton Mill. Hidden amongst a rough tangle of rock and tree within the woods is Queen's Cave, notable for its intriguing historical link with the bitter conflict of the Wars of the Roses.

Waterfall, West Dipton Wood

The Battle of Hexham and Queen's Cave

The northern lords that have forsworn thy colours,
Will follow mine, if once they see them spread;
And spread they shall be, - to thy foul disgrace,
And utter ruin of the house of York.

Queen Margaret
Henry VI Part 3 (Act 1 Scene1), William Shakespeare

Queen Margaret of Anjou was the wife of Henry VI, and due to the instability and periodic insanity of her husband she effectively became the leader of the Lancastrian cause during the Wars of the Roses. Her aim was to secure the future throne for her son Edward (destined eventually to die at the Battle of Tewkesbury).

When the head of the House of York seized the crown from her husband to become Edward IV, Margaret set about rallying her allies in the north. However, in 1464 before preparations were complete, the Lancastrian forces led by the Duke of Somerset were engaged in battle by the Neville, Lord Montague. The resulting Battle of Hexham took place on the banks of the Devil's Water, west of Linnels Bridge, and proved very one-sided with the Lancastrian army being heavily defeated. Somerset was captured, with Margaret and the young Prince Edward forced to flee. In the initial course of their flight, the queen's horse is said to have become lame at the place now known as Queen's Letch. They are then said to have sought shelter in a robber's cave deep within West Dipton Woods, which is described as consisting of two 'rooms' at the bottom of a tall sandstone crag by the West Dipton Burn.

An exploration of the shady recesses formed by the deep ravine containing West Dipton Burn (the path is rather precarious in places!) shows that there is indeed such a 'cave' feature, although it now provides limited shelter. The flaggy nature of the sandstone rock in the gorge naturally provides overhangs at several locations but nothing that could be considered substantial or comfortable. The spartan path through the woods has signs indicating that it is an old route, such as the stone posts near the start and overgrown block steps by the stream crossings. Although the hardy Queen would have had local guides and be wearily familiar with life 'on the run', the rough surroundings of West Dipton Woods certainly match much more closely with the life of a fugitive rather than privileged royalty.

As with much of history, it should be noted that there is some doubt as to the exact events that occurred. Indeed, some historians doubt whether Margaret of Anjou was even present at the Battle of Hexham, suggesting that she was elsewhere at the time, and events may possibly have become confused with a similar battle at Hedgely Moor.

Muggleswick Grange

Devil's Water, near Linnels Bridge

Upper Derwentdale at Riddlehamhope

Hexham Racecourse

Coatenhill Dam, one of the reservoirs for the Allenheads mines

The Allendales

Flow on, lovely Allen, through groves of rude grandeur,
Flow on, in thy serpentine course to the Tyne.

Anon

East and West Allendale form twin valleys draining northwards to eventually meet near Cupola. Both dales have comparable landscapes, sharing a similar natural and human history. In each case, narrow valley floors are enclosed by steep hillsides rising to broad swathes of moorland, with their valley heads topped by the expansive mass of Killhope Law (673m). Both valleys also have splendid river gorges and fine woodlands, the scenery reaching its apogee below their confluence where the River Allen flows in a spectacular gorge between Cupola and Allen Banks. The human legacy on the landscape has been especially marked by the impacts of lead mining. Although its effects have now somewhat mellowed with time, this inheritance is still quite evident around the dale heads. Although East Allendale is now more populous, this has not always been so, and there has been a substantial depopulation from the district.

At the top of East Allendale is the fascinating village of *Allenheads*, once the centre of the largest mining complex in the North Pennines and a major base for the Blackett-Beaumont business empire. The company were responsible for mine buildings, workers' housing, smelt mill and school, with their managing agent based at Allenheads Hall. Within the village neighbourhood, capped shafts and old levels hint at the vast network of underground workings below. Early workings were gradually superseded by deeper mines following a rich series of veins that converged to the east of the village towards the head of the Rookhope valley. The lead veins were also followed to the west, but the geological conditions were not as favourable there due to the presence of faulting on the Burtreeford Disturbance.

The depth of the mine workings meant that both ventilation and access became major issues. To improve ventilation, a furnace was built over one of the shafts in 1861, and the labour of using long ladders in the shafts was replaced by engine-driven man-winders or by adapted wagons that ran through the long levels. A series of reservoirs on the slopes above Allenheads (and also Corbitmere at the head of the Rookhope valley) acted as the supply for Thomas Sopwith's innovatory system of hydraulic engines in the mines. These lakes have now become popular stopover sites for migrating geese.

Allenheads in winter

Allenheads smelt mill was built north of the village near The Dodd, processing both local ore and that from upper Weardale. The vertical chimneys on the site (one of which had blown down in 1798) were replaced by a horizontal flue in 1836 that led 3km up onto the moor to a timber stack. Little is left of the mill now apart from the remains of the flue and two buildings used to store peat. Some local coal was available from the Cat Pits at the head of Allen Cleugh: as the name suggests, the raw material would not burn well on domestic fires unless mixed with clay to produce the fuel lumps known as 'cats'. Lead ore was also transported downvalley to Allen Mill and to Dukesfield Mill by the Devil's Water. In the latter case, the carriers would use the Broad Way over Hexhamshire Common, its start being clearly marked by the slanting grooves cut into the hill above Byrehope. The flat land on the crest of Byrehope Moor was also popular for horse racing.

Although Allenheads Mine employed several hundred people during the 19th century, its viability gradually declined as the workings were forced to delve deeper. Final closure in the 1890s had a major effect on the vitality of the dale. However, renewed interest arrived with the growth of fluorspar production for use in steel-making. During the 1970s, British Steel invested considerable resources in driving a new level and exploring the labyrinth of old passages to find workable fluorspar but despite this effort nothing of economic significance was found.

Nowadays, Allenheads is a much quieter place with an air of seclusion lent by the surrounding plantations of dark conifers. The Heritage Centre has a wealth of interesting information on both local history and mining in the dale, whilst the old Blackett-Beaumont school has been transformed into an Arts Centre. The reputation of Allenheads now also rests in its ample scope for outdoor activities such as walking and cycling, and it has become a key locality on the Coast-to-Coast cycle route. In winter, when snow is available, a short ski tow operates on the slopes above Allenheads Hall bringing a lively animated scene to the village.

Ropehaugh

Thomas Sopwith

The company agent for the Blackett-Beaumont mining business at Allenheads during its peak years was Thomas Sopwith. He had begun his working life as a surveyor, initially with George and Robert Stephenson on railway projects, then progressing to be a mine surveyor. As a company agent, his drive and ambition was a key factor in the improvement of technology and productivity in the mines. In particular, as a friend of William Armstrong, Sopwith developed a strong interest in the use of hydraulics for efficiently powering mechanical operations (e.g. pumping). Armstrong's key innovation had been to develop efficient pistons that used water power rather than steam power, a very important development for locations that had a better supply of rainfall than coal. Nine Armstrong hydraulic engines were supplied to Thomas Sopwith and one now remains on display adjacent to the Allenheads Heritage Centre.

A system of ten reservoirs provided the water supply for the engines, the largest being at Byrehope and Dodd, with the total supply rate being estimated at 500 horsepower. All the reservoirs were integrated into a water transfer system that supplied the Allenheads pumping engines and dressing floors before passing downvalley to further engines situated over shafts at Breckton Hill, Sipton and Holmes Linn. The water also supplied four corn-mills on the river and the two large smelt mills.

Thomas Sopwith also made radical changes in working practices and was the first to use standard mine plans. As a skilled carpenter, he also produced wooden models to illustrate key geological structures using skilfully carved inlaid and layered combinations of differently-coloured woods. These models became highly regarded and widely sought after: one is now on display at the Killhope Lead Mining Museum. His book on the mining districts of the North Pennines, published in 1833, also remains an interesting and valuable reference work.

A strong belief in good education led to the building of new schools at both Sinderhope and Allenheads, and from his home at Allenheads Hall Sopwith could observe and reprimand malingerers. Contemporary reports suggest that the illiteracy rate was only about 10% in the dale, whereas it reached 36% in the coalfield areas to the east, although this also reflects the imperative given to education by lead-mining families.

However, Sopwith also had a reputation as being rather ruthless with those that opposed him: he refused to employ striking miners that would not accept his new working practices, eventually forcing them to leave the dale or even emigrate. As with many eminent Victorians he was also a very good self-publicist and some of his successes relied somewhat fortuitously on the high lead price at the time.

In the valley below Allenheads are the rows of cottages at Dirt Pot and Ropehaugh, also built by the Blackett-Beaumont company. Despite their small population, they were served by the traditional two Methodist chapels, one for the Wesleyan branch and the other for Primitive Methodists. Also located here is the old Candle House which supplied the miners with their underground lighting.

A little further downvalley, opposite the small cluster of houses at Spartylea, is the side-valley of Swinhope. During the bitter miners' strike of 1849, when Thomas Sopwith introduced his contested changes in working practices, the chapel at Swinhope became a meeting place for the strikers. Some of those who were subsequently forced to leave the dale emigrated and settled in the United States, founding there the settlement of Galena, Ohio. The old lead mine at Swinhopehead was re-opened in the 1960s to unsuccessfully explore for zinc ore southwards under Killhope Law.

At the foot of the Swinhope valley, limestone emerges conspicuously at Elpha Green and there are some cave passages in the outcrops (the 'Elf Holes'), but access has been complicated by rock falls. The kilns at Swinhope, and those nearer Allenheads at Slag Hill, are relics of agricultural lime-burning: at least eighteen such kilns existed in the valley.

By the river, near to Spartylea, stand the remains of the old corn mill and the quaint old chapel of St. Peter's which was rebuilt in the early 19th century. A short distance downstream at Sipton are the ruins of the large ore-dressing plant established by the Blackett-Beaumont company, which was heavily damaged by a large fire in 1929. Sipton also has one of the deep shafts sunk on the famous Blackett Level (p.116), the shaft being later used by the Weardale Lead Company to raise ore from the veins cut by the level. The nearby St. Peter's Mine operated during the 20th century after the Blackett Level reached this point in 1901, prior to its final termination close by. Recently, this mine has been utilised to obtain high-quality specimens of fluorite for the mineral-collecting market.

Beyond the short terrace of miners' cottages at Sipton, larch plantations become prominent components of the valley scenery. Usually the plantations are dark and shady features, but in late autumn the trees become transformed by their deciduous needles, colouring the dale with a vivid golden-honey hue. Larch and fir plantations were planted by the mining companies to be harvested and used in the mines, particularly for beams and props.

At a higher level, above the valley sides, are the expansive moorlands of Allendale Common and Hexhamshire Common. Both of these upland areas remain unenclosed, unlike the compartmentalized valley intakes, and this is apparently one of the legacies of the Blackett-Beaumont landowners who wished to preserve their sporting interests there.

Lime kilns at Slaghill, with Killhope Law beyond

Swinhope

Near to Sinderhope, the river encounters a bed of limestone, forming a twisting gorge headed by the beautiful cascade of *Holmes Linn*. The Linn presents a scene of great charm, for much of the year a charming combination of falling water and dappled foliage. Adjacent to the fall is another of the shafts sunk on the Blackett Level, which indicates that the outlook here was not always one of peaceful tranquillity. The large water wheel located over this shaft was later transported to Upper Weardale where it became the now-celebrated 'Killhope Wheel'.

The Blackett Level

Thomas Sopwith's most ambitious project was the construction of the Blackett Level, a grandiose long-term scheme that only a large company could have countenanced or afforded. The intention was both to develop an effective drainage system for the mines in the valley and to explore new ground at depth. Work on the level began at Allendale Town in 1855 with a series of shafts then sunk upon its projected course and the level also driven in each direction from their base. These intermediate shafts at Breckton Hill, Sipton, Holmes Linn and Studdon utilised Sopwith's system of hydraulic engines for pumping and ventilation.

The original scheme envisioned extending the level for 11km to Allenheads, but ultimately only two-thirds of this distance was achieved. When work finally ended in 1905, the final cost was in excess of £120,000. Five veins were intersected by the level, of which three were quite productive, but these did not repay the vast investment. History shows that the level was driven too late to reach the deep workings at Allenheads before the precipitous collapse of the industry in the late 19th century.

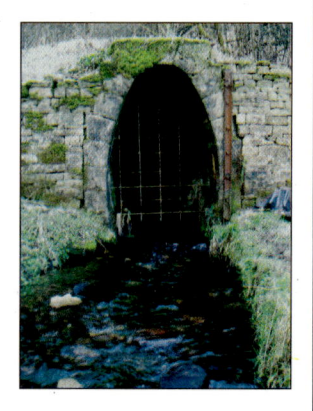

Holmes Linn

The main settlement in the dale is *Allendale Town* (originally known as 'Allenton'), where the houses are centred upon a spacious market place. The town has a long history, with its first charter having been awarded by Edward I in the 13th century. During the lead-mining boom it became the centre of economic activity for both of the Allendales, with the population peaking at 6500 in the 19th century. In those times, the bustling market place would be particularly hectic during the twice-yearly event of 'the Pays' when the miners received any money due on closing their 'bargains' with the company. The wealth of the town was demonstrated during the 1851 Great Exhibition at Crystal Palace when Allendale sent a silver ingot weighing 345kgs.

Nowadays the town is best-known for the annual *'Tar Barling'* festival held on New Year's Eve. Locally this is 'Old Year's Night' with a procession of 'guizers' carrying blazing tar barrels around the town accompanied by a brass band, followed by the igniting of a large bonfire fuelled by the tar barrels. The ceremony has distant origins in ancient Celtic fire rituals which were commonplace in pagan times, celebrating key events in the ancient calendar.

To the south-west of Allendale Town, there is an interesting group of buildings at Wooley, arranged in a strategic cluster around a triangular-shaped yard. Their origin is defensive, containing two bastle-type fortified buildings and possibly the earlier traces of a traditional Northumbrian single-storey 'longhouse' that would have accommodated both people and cattle within the same dwelling. The cluster of buildings suggests that this was the focal point for one of the most important farms in the district. More than forty bastles have been recorded in this parish, many of which have now been adapted into more comfortable modern buildings or used as outhouses. Other interesting examples can be found to north and east of Allendale Town including those at Old Town, Housty and Moor House, whilst to the south a similar type of building exists at Sinderhope Shield.

A short distance downstream from Mill Bridge (site of the old corn mill serving Allendale Town) is the ruined winding house and arched entrance to the *Blackett Level*. Stone arching was normal around level entrances, providing extra support for the adit in the looser rocks near the surface, whilst deep underground it was not normally required except where rocks were fractured or unstable.

A little further downriver is Allen Mill, former site of a large smelting complex and now rather derelict. The smelt mill replaced an earlier site downstream with the riverside location ensuring a plentiful water supply. Ore processing capacity was steadily built up over the 18th and 19th centuries, so that by its peak period the mill had two calcining furnaces, five roasting furnaces, two reverberatory furnaces, two reducing furnaces, eight ore hearths, two slag hearths and a separating house with pots for refining silver. Smelting was a highly skilled activity: if the temperature was too low or too high then valuable metal would be wasted. Evidence from the parish records indicates that in the early years of operation, skilled smelters came to Allendale from Derbyshire in order to optimise the operations at the mill.

Originally two tall chimneys stood on-site, but these proved inadequate: in most weather conditions, the valley floor situation would not have encouraged dispersal of the toxic fumes. Therefore work was begun in 1807 on a large flue which led 1km up the hill to an outlet at Cleugh Head. Despite the considerable horizontal length, this also proved inadequate, and the flue was then extended much further up the hill in 1837 with another major flue also being constructed nearby. The total lengths of these twin flues therefore became more than 4km making them the longest such features in the North Pennines. Although the flues have mainly disappeared from the lower pastures, the higher sections on the moor remain mainly intact and exhibit the construction quality of the turf-covered stone arching. Quarries at Fell Head indicate where the stone for the flues was excavated and shaped by masons. Both flues have occasional entrances where the young worker lads would enter the dark noxious condensing chambers in order to remove the lead residues.

The Allen Mill chimneys on Flow Moss

The Allen Mill flues terminate at two large chimneys on Flow Moss that are prominent landmarks throughout much of the surrounding area. The track leading past the chimneys is a section of carriers' way used for the transport of ore from West Allendale to the smelt mill. Of the two chimneys, the most westerly is the more massive, 30m in circumference, and this acted as a conduit for both flues. One of the flues also initially used the other chimney, which is taller but has a smaller circumference. When the mill was in full working operation, these chimneys would have belched out large plumes of smoke and fumes that would have identified the Allendales from a considerable distance away. The mill finally closed in 1896 as the industry rapidly declined, but the chimneys and flues now serve as fitting monuments to the efforts and ingenuity of the local miners.

Carriers' Ways and 'Galloway Trods'

The Broad Way, Black Way and Carriers' Way crossing the Allendale moors are good examples of the old packhorse routes used for transporting mine material and other commercial produce. Often referred to as 'galloway trods' after the sturdy little packhorses used by the carriers (although jaeger ponies or 'jaggers' were also common), they provided reliable tracks for delivering ore to the smelt mills or to take the finished lead to market in the Tyne valley. Regular use of the trods sometimes meant that paving or a raised surface (known as a 'causey') was laid across swampy places for ease of movement, but even with such aids, movement often came to a halt during the difficult conditions of winter.

Each packhorse would carry two balanced loads weighing about one hundredweight (102kgs), either twin 'pokes' of ore or 'pigs' of lead. These loads were carried either in panniers or baskets supported on a wooden frame ('crutch'). A train of 20-30 horses would be formed with a bell-horse at the front and a heeler dog at the rear to keep them moving. Horses were usually fitted with muzzles as some of the grazing was poisoned by smelter fumes, such as on Flow Moss.

Relationships between the carriers and the lead mining companies were frequently difficult. When the price of lead was high and the company wanted to get as much material to market as possible, the carriers would bargain for higher rates, sometimes abandoning one load for a more lucrative contract and then retrieving it later. However, at other times when the price was low, the company would stockpile their lead meaning that there would be less work for the carriers. With the general road improvements in the North Pennines during the 19th century (much of it subsidised by the large mining companies) and the introduction of turnpikes, the power of the carriers decreased further and their businesses gradually disappeared.

Carriers' Way from Weardale to Allenheads

To the north of Allen Mill, on the road leading up to the large village of Catton, is the terminus of the disused railway that formerly linked with Hexham. This railway line opened quite late compared to others in adjacent valleys, and at a time when the lead-mining 'boom' was past its peak, therefore it never reached its intended destination at Allenheads. As levels of use therefore did not grow as had been anticipated, the railway was closed to passengers in 1930 and then to freight in 1950.

The route of the railway line followed the valley of the East Allen north-west from Catton, diverging from the main road (B6295) which leads over the hill to Langley (p.127). Catton Beacon provides a fine view of the lower dale and surrounding area, and was once the site of the traditional beacon to warn of impending trouble from the north but is now crowned instead by prominent masts. Passengers on the old railway line would have had a good prospect of the attractively-wooded lower course of the River East Allen, which flows swiftly past Oakpool and Wide Eals to eventually merge at Water Meetings (Cupola) with its twin stream, the River West Allen. A pleasant and secluded path follows this last section of the river through pastures and meadow.

*From the far off southern rim
Where the hills loom dark and grim
West All'n Water fair yet bleak
Downward flows a silver streak*
                    Joseph Ritson, 1921

West Allendale is a quiet and secluded backwater these days. The busy road from the Tyne Valley to Alston (A696) passes through the well-wooded lower dale and offers a glimpse of a green valley curving between sombre fells, but few venture this way. In the words of Joseph Ritson, it is 'fair yet bleak', the balance usually varying depending on the season or distance up the dale. However, quite remarkably, back in the later half of the 19th century, more than 500 miners were employed by the Blackett-Beaumont company in West Allendale. At that time there was considerably more activity on the roads and byways, and the tiny remnant settlements of today had a function as busy villages.

The most intense activity was at Coalcleugh, located at the head of the dale in a fold of the bleak moors. The situation at 530m above sea-level is open and exposed, overlooked by the broad swelling domes of Killhope Law (673m) and The Dodd (614m). As the scale of the surface heaps imply, Coalcleugh lead mine worked the same rich veins that were also found over the fell in the adjacent Nent valley, eventually linking underground with that valley. During the 18th century, the mine was reputed to be the deepest in England and it has a history of innovation. The development of the Coalcleugh Level became the first underground use of a horse-drawn wagon way, and it also pioneered the use of iron-capped rails in levels and the installation of one of the first hydraulic engines. Water power was provided by a reservoir at Coalcleugh Dam on the fellside to the south. The mine was the biggest employer in the dale, with 200-300 men underground in the 19th century. After the main phase of lead mining had ended, the Vieille Montagne Company took over the lease and worked it mainly for zinc ore until 1921. In addition, as the place-name Coalcleugh suggests, coal is also present here with surface pits and spoil indicating working of that narrow seam.

Many of the buildings around Coalcleugh are now derelict, but hark back to the days when miners eked a dual-living from farming in order to supplement their fluctuating mining incomes. A few sturdy dwellings remain, now transformed into comfortable houses despite the exposed situation. Rush-covered grooves of 'galloway trods' traverse the moors, indicating the old routes to the smelt mills. The Black Way leads over the fell to East Allendale, whilst another carriers' route follows the ridge of The Dodd and Middle Rigg heading for Whitfield Mill lower down West Allendale.

Desolation.........Coalcleugh in winter

Serenity.........Coalcleugh in summer

West Allendale

Further mining remains are evident downvalley at *Carrshield*, which also has a long history of underground activity dating back to the 1760s. Here the Blackett-Beaumont company developed Scraithole Mine, which was in use through the 19th century and linked with workings in the Wellhope valley to the west where good zinc ore was found (Wellhope was also linked with Nentsberry Haggs mine in the Nent valley). Scraithole was later re-opened in the 1970s and 1980s to explore for reserves of the mineral *witherite*, which although relatively common around Allendale, is extremely rare elsewhere throughout the world.

The most conspicuous remains today are those of the two-storied lodging 'shop', representing the largest of its type in the North Pennines, but there are other interesting relics including ruined bousesteems, culverts, arched level entrances and a rail system. The river banks have been revetted to constrain its flow of water and provide space for the dressing floors that occupied the base of the valley. Many of the buildings at Carrshield were built by the Blackett-Beaumont company for its workers, including the prominent school. However, the ruined structure at Whitely Shield is much older, being the ruins of a late 16th century bastle.

At Carrshield, the austere outlook characterising the upper reaches of West Allendale begins to soften. A patchwork mosaic of enclosed pasture-land is complemented by groups of trees that shade the river banks. A little further downvalley, limestone makes its distinctive appearance and the river dashes into an attractive gorge near Wolfcleugh. The river bed is frequently pitted and fretted by solution features, the scenery having many similarities with that of Holmes Linn in East Allendale. The fortuitous position of nearby Limestone Brae is signified by its name, with the emerald-green fields and flowery glades by the stream indicating more fertile lime-rich soils. Small limestone quarries are found on the upper slopes and were associated with kilns used to produce agricultural lime, notably at Ninebanks and Hesleywell.

The prominent Methodist chapel at Limestone Brae is one of many in the dale with ten being built in just this one parish: John Wesley had included Allendale on his preaching tours of the country in the 18th century. Other interesting chapels in the vicinity include those at High House, Carrshield and Appletree Shield, whilst the main parish church is at Ninebanks. With the different branches of Methodism eventually reunifying in 1932 and the decline in rural populations, many chapels have become redundant buildings. Happily many have survived intact by being modified for other uses such as village halls or for residential use, so retaining an active presence in the local community. Nowadays, the religious diversity in West Allendale is further enhanced by a Buddhist abbey located on the hill near to Limestone Brae.

Mine 'shop', Carrshield

River West Allen, near Limestone Brae

In the vicinity of *Ninebanks*, the river is joined by the Mohope Burn, another large stream from the west draining the two upland valleys of Mohope and Wellhope. Both of these valleys were important mining sites in the past as clearly indicated by the deep 'hushes' that have disturbed the ground, most notably near to the youth hostel. Nowadays this area is virtually deserted, but in medieval times there were villages at Keirsleywell Row and Hesleywell, and this was followed by the influx of miners in the 18th and 19th centuries. Although the present-day road to Alston (A686) proceeds over Whitfield Moor, the old way was through the Mohope valley via Blacklaw Cross, this being a key section of the historic route from Penrith to Corbridge.

Ninebanks also has a distinctive late-medieval pele tower that is unusual in having four storeys (the raising of the road has put the basement below ground-level). The tower was developed as a defensive part of the adjacent manor house, with the top storey and stair turret being later 16th century additions. At Keirsleywell Row, there are also parts of a 17th century bastle at Furnace House, although the original building has apparently later been extended in association with early lead smelting activities. Farms in this part of the valley have conspicuous 'hemmels' (partly-covered cattle yards) leading directly onto the road.

Ninebanks Tower

West Allendale near Hesleywell

122

Although the upper section of West Allendale can be bleak at times, the lower parts of the valley are undoubtedly rather attractive, becoming well-wooded with a notable variety of trees. This is part of the large Whitfield estate which has its centre at the large manor house of Whitfield Hall, established on the site of an older tower-house in 1785: the hall is particularly noted for its fine gardens. Nearby are the small group of buildings at Bearsbridge, including an inn, and the dispersed houses and church that make up the hamlet of Whitfield itself. Amongst these is the Old Town of Whitfield, hidden away in a small cluster by the Church Burn. On the east bank of the river, Monk's Wood provides a particularly interesting and diverse setting, with a rich woodland flora. Higher up the same slopes above the deep valley is the flatter area of Keenley Fell, where there are more limestone quarries and kilns.

The buildings at Monk and Burnlaw both contain interesting defensive relics from the past. As its name suggests, Monk was an outlying 'cell' associated with the priory of Hexham and 16th century records refer to it as 'le Menke'. The group of buildings at Monk seems to include four distinct bastle-type buildings of different ages, with the oldest to the south, in addition to a dovecote. An unusual local sect called the Bochimites (after a biblical passage in Judges ii, 5) was later founded in this vicinity by Francis Swindle of Dryburn. It was mainly a reaction against perceived injustices amongst the Wesleyian Methodists and, as with many such sects, ultimately disappeared with the death of its founder.

At *Cupola*, the two branches of the River Allen unite to enter a deep gorge which extends for 5km to the Tyne Valley. The unusual place-name is derived from the revolutionary lead-smelting 'cupola' furnace installed at nearby Whitfield Mill by the London Lead Company, which was one of the first to use the superior reverberation method to concentrate heat whilst roasting the ore. Eventually this smelt mill was superseded by that established at Nenthead and it closed in 1821 with very little remaining of it today.

The elegant stone arches of Cupola Bridge date from the late 18th century and carry the Alston-Hexham road (A686) over the expanding river. The steep slopes on the eastern side of the bridge are negotiated by the road through a wide alpine-style 'hairpin' (traditionally known as the Grindstone Elbow).

Downstream of the bridge, the river loops through the deep sinuous curves of the Crooks of Allen, overlooked by broken crags and vertiginous woodland. After the initial easy section below the bridge, rough paths perched on the steep valley sides provide the only access to this spectacular scene, except for the canoeists' approach of taking to the water and shooting the rapids and eddies of the river! Amongst these rapids is Cyphers Linn, where the river cascades over a series of steps into a system of deep pools.

Cupola Bridge

High above the Allen gorge, on a lofty beldevere, are the ruins of *Staward Pele*. Its situation is particularly impressive, with a narrow ridge-crest forming a slender tongue of elevated land separating the deep gorge of the River Allen from the ravine of Harsondale Cleugh. At the abrupt end of this ridge, the stronghold of Staward Pele was located in an optimal defensive position from which to repel invaders from the north and thereby protect the entrance to the Allendales.

The main ruins seen today are of the stone keep and gatehouse built in the 14th century. Both the keep and the courtyard were enclosed by a thick curtain wall with ditch around the summit of the ridge: access could therefore only be gained through the gatehouse tower from the south-east. Some of the well-dressed stone in the gatehouse appears to have been re-used from a Roman temple which had previously existed on the site. When its role as a defensive fortress had passed, the site became a place of prayer for monks from the Priory of Hexham. In the 17th century, James I granted the building to Lord Howard de Weldon who dismantled much of the stonework, using it to build Staward Manor in a more comfortable location. This accounts for its present ruinous state and also the apparent removal of Roman altar relics for use as a quoin (keystone). Local legend also suggests that a pot of gold from the site was lost in a deep pool of the river near Cyphers Linn. Rather ironically, considering its original purpose, the ruined fortress afterwards became a favoured hideaway for Dickey of Kingswood, a notorious Border Reiver.

Downstream the gorge opens out into a clearing at Plankey Mill with a rustic suspension bridge crossing the river in traditional rickety fashion. This is followed by a dramatic final section where the river cuts a tempestuous course directly through the last hill blocking its exit to the Tyne valley. Here are the famous *Allen Banks* which are threaded by numerous paths, both low-level by the river, or at a higher level climbing up to impressive viewpoints. On the west bank, a track leads up by the Hoods Burn to the unusual setting of the Bone Floor, part of a summer house created by Susan Davidson of Ridley Hall in the 19th century. The design is rather unusual with a floor composed of tightly-packed sheep bones (intended to keep the floor dry) enclosed by flagstones. On the east bank, another steep climb reveals the hidden fairy pond of Moralee Tarn, embowered in its small hollow by lush woodland. In spring, the aroma of wild garlic fills the air whilst in autumn the array of changing colours is complemented by a wealth of exotic fungi.

The gorge abruptly ends at Ridley Hall near another suspension bridge, and the river debouches onto the wide and flat valley floor of the South Tyne. There is a large car park here that is inevitably popular and was formerly the walled garden of the neo-Tudor-style country hall (now adapted into a residential and conference centre). The ancient home of the Ridleys was 3km west at the impressive pele-tower of Willimoteswick, part of which dates back to the 11th century. Nearer to Ridley Hall is the charming hamlet of Beltingham, a particularly attractive grouping of old houses centred on the historic 16th century church of St. Cuthbert.

Staward Gorge and Allen Banks

Where can you find a fairer sight
By noon or eve or morning light
Than Catton's lofty height has shown
Or Staward, peerless beauty's throne
Joseph Ritson 1921

The deep gorge through which the lower River Allen flows is justly celebrated for its cornucopia of wonderful scenery. Much of the land is owned by the National Trust and a plethora of popular paths weave through the area. Throughout the gorge, the river banks are extravagantly wooded, especially on the steepest slopes where vertical foliage cascades over rocky crags. The result is a romantic blend of rushing waters, glorious woodlands and dramatic winding paths. Flora and fauna are also varied and profuse, with the woods becoming carpeted by bluebells in spring. Dippers can frequently be seen darting in and out of the river, and the woods remain one of the last Pennine refuges of the red squirrel.

Allen Banks from Gingle Pot

Kingswood and Staward Gorge

Langley Mill chimney on Stublick Moor

John Martin

The scenery of Allendale was a major influence on the extraordinary early 19th century painter John Martin, who was born in nearby Haydon Bridge. After studying art, he moved to London in 1806, and began to produce his grandiose canvases, inspired both by biblical passages and his native landscape. His great celestial landscape *'The Plains of Heaven'*, now in the Tate Gallery (London), is thought to have its roots in the Allendale scenery. In addition, *'The Bard'*, which now hangs in the Laing Gallery of Newcastle, appears to draw heavily on the location of Staward Pele. In his time, Martin became hugely popular, influencing many writers and artists of the time including the Brontes, Keats and Victor Hugo; French Romantic writers invented the word *'Martinien'* to describe spectacular or exaggerated scenes. Ultimately, however, tastes changed and the rise of other artists such as Turner and Constable, together with sustained attacks by critics such as John Ruskin, meant his popularity declined. Nevertheless, his epic visions have retained many admirers and a painting today could sell for millions of pounds.

East of Staward Gorge and Allen Banks, the dominating landmark is the sentinel chimney on Stublick Moor, which was the terminus of a flue running from nearby *Langley Mill*. The availability of good local coal from Stublick Colliery and proximity to the Tyne valley meant that this was an optimal site for lead smelting, despite the distance from the mining areas. Two separate mills were built here, the first being constructed in 1768 by the Greenwich Hospital Commissioners to smelt the levy ore they obtained from mines leased upon their land. In 1822 this mill employed 50 men smelting lead and 6 men smelting zinc, but shortly afterwards zinc production was discontinued due to a fall in price. The second mill was established by Jopling & Company who worked the lead veins at Blagill on Alston Moor, and it had a similar capacity (about 12,000 pieces per annum). Water supply for the mills was a problem, initially overcome by an aqueduct, then by the adjacent reservoir that is popular with fishermen today.

The horizontal flue and chimney were originally built by the agents James and Peter Mulcaster to remove toxic fumes from the site, but it was eventually realised that when the fumes condensed in the wider parts of the flue, the resultant residue would have a significant economic value. This led to the construction of other horizontal flues elsewhere in the region and the employment of many small boys to clear out their residues. Another virtue of the mill was that, when it was eventually constructed, the Allendale to Hexham railway line passed the site. By that time, however, business was declining and the mill finally closed in 1887.

The impressive edifice of *Langley Castle* was extensively modified in the 19th century, but the uncompromising format of the original building can still be readily appreciated. It was built about 1350 as one of a chain of fortresses guarding the vulnerable Tyne valley and has a very distinctive tall and compact structure. The central section is surrounded by four massive square towers each rising by an extra stage higher than it. By the 16th century, the castle was in ruins and although the remedial work means that little remains of the original interior, the exterior remains essentially true to its medieval form. The building now operates as a hotel and function centre.

Crooks of Allen

Langley Castle

Hexhamshire Common from Sinderhope Carr

South Tynedale at Garrigill

South Tynedale

Pent in a narrow valley, over which mountains frowned with melancholy sterility and nakedness .... where all the earth produces from its bowels, and where the people also are so generally subterranean.

Alston from *A History of Cumberland*, William Hutchison 1794

From its source at Tyne Head springs, the River South Tyne strikes a distinctive northerly course until its broad sweep eastwards near Haltwhistle. The river's name comes from an old Celtic word 'ti' or 'tei' meaning simply 'to flow' and the noble valley formed by the river is commonly referred to as South Tynedale. In the past, this valley formed the southern sector of the old liberty of Tynedale, once a territory of the Scottish kings. At the head of the dale, the huge bulk of Cross Fell is the dominating feature, whilst lower down are fertile pastures and rich woodlands enclosed by steep valley sides and rather bleak moorland. Occasional settlements occur throughout the valley but many dwellings tend to be scattered and dispersed. For much of its course, the river flows in broad gravelly ribbons amongst the valley *haughs*. This is one of the legacies resulting from an extensive mining industry that once existed in the upper reaches of the catchment.

Alston naturally acts as the focal point for the valley, strategically situated where the major tributary of the River Nent joins the South Tyne: its name being derived from the older version 'Aldenestone' (probably meaning 'Aldwin's town'). A series of high-level routes radiate from here, crossing the fells to the Eden valley, Teesdale and Weardale. Part of the town's charm lies in the lack of a formal plan for its buildings, with houses being haphazardly arranged on the valley slopes in an eclectic mix of rows, tiers and odd clusters, threaded by steep cobbled streets and narrow alleyways. The cobbles are from a local source, the flagstone quarry high on Flinty Fell. Many of the old buildings exhibit distinction and character, and a common feature is for the elevated townhouses to have steps leading directly to the first floor. Inns and public houses are also conspicuous, although the number of such buildings has decreased from a remarkable twenty-three in 1847 to a more sober seven premises now. The prominent spire of St. Augustine's Church dates from the late 19th century and replaced an earlier design created by the famous engineer John Smeaton (who also built the *Nentforce Level*: p.135).

Although markets are now held infrequently, the town has an established status as the highest market town in England. The 18th century market cross, with sheltering roof supported by sturdy pillars, was donated by local-born William Stephenson who became Mayor of London in 1764. Unfortunately the cross has twice required rebuilding after having been damaged by lorries struggling with the steep gradients of the High Street. Behind the Market Place is High Mill, an old corn mill still retaining its wheelhouse (complete with wheel) and open to the public. Narrow lanes provide access from the market area to the River Nent with its attractive waterfalls and the popular Gossipgate walks. The land around The Butts was formerly the zone utilised for compulsory archery practice. Down by the South Tyne at Townfoot is one of the few areas of level ground where the river floodplain has formed a broad terrace used as a recreation area.

Alston from the west

Mining at Alston Moor

Alston Moor has long been famous for its rich mineral lodes and the surrounding uplands bear many signs of the efforts made to extract these abundant resources. Although no direct evidence of Roman involvement has been found, the fort that they built at Whitley Castle (2.5km north-west of Alston) suggests an interest in the early mines. Pieces of lead ore and slag found at the fort have a high silver content indicating they were probably derived from stream deposits in the Garrigill area.

When Tynedale passed into control of the Scottish kingdom (although nominally considered to be in England), which pertained until the reign of Edward I, the mineral rights continued to be held by the English Crown. Old coins unearthed at Browngill Mine in the 19th century were found to contain the imprint of the English king William II (1087-1100) but the Scottish king David I (1124-1153) also apparently used the Alston district as a source for his mint.

The high silver content placed the mines within the Royal prerogative, hence their association with the renowned 'Silver Mines of Carlisle'. This explains the detaching of Alston from Northumberland and its incorporation into Cumberland in the mid-12th century. Under this royal licence, German mining experts and merchants became involved in the industry, and at a later stage specialists also came north from Derbyshire. This activity is reflected in the abundance of 'Old Man' workings at Alston Moor, usually shallow workings such as open-cuts or line shafts based upon veins exposed in nearby streams.

From the early 18th century, mineral rights became the property of the person owning the soil and this encouraged a strong entrepreneurial spirit. The Earl of Derwentwater forfeited his large estates in the area and the Royal Hospital for Seamen at Greenwich became the major landowner. An exception was the Liberty of Priorsdale which had belonged to the Priory of Hexham and was then passed on for sale separately.

During the late 18th century, mining leases for much of the Greenwich Hospital land and for Priorsdale were gained by the London Lead Company and they set about a co-ordinated development of the area with a major base at Nenthead. Leases for some of the veins, however, continued to remain with smaller companies. Varying duties were payable to Greenwich Hospital, typically a fifth or a sixth of the ore, but in rich areas as much as a third was required. During most of the 19th century there were over 100 lead mines operating on Alston Moor, and by 1821 the Greenwich Hospital had an annual income in excess of £100,000. As elsewhere, the London Lead Company had a particularly positive impact on education in the parish: in 1805, 209 children received schooling, but by 1822 this had risen to about 1000.

When the mining industry entered its steep decline in the late 19th century, the London Lead Company left the area, and there was much local poverty together with out-migration. Some of the leases eventually passed to the Belgian company Vieille Montagne who redeveloped the mines in the early 20th century, especially for zinc. Since then, there have been various other small operations, but nothing of real significance compared to the scale of previous activity. In some of the mines, small amounts of ochre have also been extracted for use in pigments. All the mines are now closed although some interest remains in the zinc reserves.

Curiously, old writings often portray Alstonians as being rather unusual! In addition to Hutchison's description (p.129), another example is from the 1829 Parson & White trade directory for Cumberland which provides the following description:

'Most of the men are miners, and by long continuance in the works they show a simplicity of manners rarely found among other labouring people; they are strong of limb, and when in liquor, a vice too frequent, they are quarrelsome and resolute; but when from home, are remarkably tractable, and steadfastly attached to their countrymen and fellow labourers.'

Westgarth Forster and William Wallace

Westgarth Forster was a very influential figure both at Alston Moor and throughout the North Pennines on account of his seminal work from 1809 entitled *'A Treatise on a Section of the Strata from Newcastle-upon-Tyne to Cross Fell'*. Earlier he had been managing agent for the Blackett-Beaumont company from 1797-1807, following on from the death of his father in the same position.

Forster left the company to pursue new directions, including the publication of his famous book that, despite its rather convoluted title, represented a masterly synthesis of the geology of the region, including the disposition of the mineral veins and mining developments. This *magnum opus* soon became a key reference document and ran to three major editions. The third edition (revised by the Rev. W. Nall) was particularly influential because it integrated the distinctive names used by miners and quarrymen into the general geological sequence (e.g. *slaty hazle, four fathom limestone, grindstone sill* etc.).

After publication of his book, Forster became a mine surveyor and consultant, travelling worldwide. However, despite his great knowledge, and some notable successes, other speculative mining ventures proved rather unsuccessful. As a result, by the time of his death in 1835, he had become almost destitute. He is buried in the churchyard at Garrigill.

The 19th century contemporary writings of William Wallace have also provided an important record of the momentous events of the time. He lived and worked for many years at Alston Moor during the latter part of the century, with an inquisitive mind that accumulated a detailed knowledge of its geology and history. Wallace published material on both these aspects, notably a detailed account of the formation of lead veins in 1861 and a fascinating history and account of local life in 1890 (*'Alston Moor: its Pastoral People, its Mines and Miners'*).

To the south of Alston, the lovely village of *Garrigill* lies at the head of the South Tyne valley, forming an attractive group of houses with inn and church around a spacious village green. As with the other villages of Alston Moor, Garrigill's history is strongly associated with mining, the population reaching 1540 people in 1824. Pasture land continues a short distance beyond the village to a scattering of farmhouses at Dorthgill and Tynehead, but the fells gradually close in on the narrowing valley giving it the impression of a green oasis amidst a sombre brown and ochre backdrop.

The Pennine Way and the cyclists' Coast-to-Coast variation route descend to lower ground at Garrigill after crossing the fells from the Eden valley. As a result, the village green is often strewn with recuperating bodies and the 'George and Dragon' continues to do good business! Both these itineraries utilise the so-called 'corpse road' over the high flanks of Cross Fell, a route by which the deceased from Garrigill were said to be taken for a Christian burial at Kirkland in the Eden valley before consecrated land became locally available. However, the evidence for this practice is uncertain, being based mainly upon anecdotes collected by the 19th century writer William Wallace, although it is worth noting that there was an ecclesiastical dispute with Alston for a while. The anecdotal accounts told of one notable occasion when a blinding snowstorm caused the coffin party to abandon their load on the fell and seek refuge back in the valley, returning some time later to complete their task.

The main road from Teesdale (B6277) reaches the head of the South Tyne valley by the high remote pass of Yad Moss. Ski tows adorn the flanks of Burnhope Seat near the road, and this normally quiet fellside can become a considerable hive of activity when a good snowfall blankets the slopes. The B6277 road does not actually descend to the valley floor or go through Garrigill itself, but keeps to a higher shelf instead all the way to Alston. The road therefore crosses a series of streams descending to the infant South Tyne that have each carved their own impressive ravines, with the most remarkable of these being Ash Gill about 1km south-east of Garrigill.

The upper section of Ash Gill drains the lonely upland territory of Priorsdale, formerly a district of the priory of Hexham; the local freeholders initially resisted the land becoming incorporated within Alston Moor as they feared the loss of the liberties granted by the priory. One of the houses (now no longer inhabited) in this side-valley has been given the rather apt name of Seldom Seen. Ash Gill then descends to pass below an impressive bridge on the B6277 road, before abruptly dropping over a sheer limestone cliff to form the spectacular waterfall of *Ashgill Force* (photo: p.8).

An active day at the ski tows above Yad Moss

Priorsdale House: 'four square walls to the wind' at an elevation of 540m

Icicles in Ash Gill

Both Ashgill Force and the impressive gorge below are easily accessible from the road, but also make a very pleasant short excursion from Garrigill. The overhanging lip over which the stream cascades means that it is even possible to admire the scene from behind the waterfall too, although this can become rather perilous in some conditions: in winter, icicles of Damoclean proportions can build up here. In the amphitheatre beneath the fall are some ruined bouseteems indicating that this site was once used for washing lead ore mined from nearby levels.

Below the Force, the stream then drops over a staircase of additional falls in very beautiful surroundings, rushing down to join the South Tyne. The scene is often further enlivened by the resident dipper flitting busily from pool to pool. In the downvalley direction towards Alston are other interesting gorges that are worth exploring, notably Thorter Gill and Nattrass Gill, each of which contains sparkling cascades and attractive woodlands.

Poignant overgrown ruins are the most visible legacy left by mining in the Garrigill area, notably the series of abandoned old buildings at Tynehead. The mines are recorded as having been worked since at least the 13th century, although probably operating much earlier. The mineral veins were not particularly rich in lead compared to others elsewhere on Alston Moor, but some had an unusually high silver content. Zinc carbonate ore (*smithsonite* or 'calamine') was also mined and traces of gold are even said to have been found at Tynehead.

The Whin Sill cuts across the South Tyne valley hereabouts, and the river has cut a gorge through it to form the impressive double waterfall of Tyne Force, with another fine fall on the adjacent stream of Clar Gill. Another remarkable feature that may be noticed in this part of the valley is the Great Sulphur Vein which the old miners called the 'Backbone of the Earth' because its large up-fold of rocks (in places up to 400m wide) seemed to them to expose the bare bones of the planet. Although this vein contains no significant lead ore, it is often very conspicuous in the local landscape on account of its sparkling quartz crystals. Its prominence apparently also attracted Welsh and Derbyshire miners to this remote location looking for copper, but although both copper pyrite *(chalcopyrite)* and iron pyrite ('fool's gold') are present, none of the required mineral was concentrated enough to have an economic value.

Above Tynehead, there were further important mines at Calvert and Tynegreen, of which only crumbling ruins remain. These relics are situated near to the springs marking the source of the River South Tyne which is now marked by a distinctly modern stone sculpture. The London Lead Company built the road that leads past these mines and through to the upper Tees at Moor House: it then linked with the high remote workings on Dufton Fell.

Pasture Houses and Garrigill

Tyne Force

Sillyhall, between Garrigill and Alston

'Greg's Hut' on the Pennine Way at the site of the old Crossfell mine

At Garrigill, the Tynebottom Mine fortuitously found a locality where the veins had opened out horizontally into lateral 'flats'. This meant that the amount of ore available was significantly increased. The spoil heaps from this mine have become a happy hunting ground for mineral collectors because of the unusual specimens available. Similarly the hillsides above the main road to Alston are also scored by old mine workings. This is especially noticeable where the minor road branches off over the fell to Nenthead, with lines of shafts indicating the rich Browngill and Browngill Sun Veins (the latter so named because it is to the south of the main vein): these extensive workings cross the watershed to link up with those at Nenthead.

Luck and knowledge were undoubtedly two key factors dictating the path of a miner's life. This is clearly shown by Utrick Walton's discovery of the Crag Green veins, near Garrigill, which happened when runoff from a thunderstorm eroded away the overlying vegetation. Walton was quick to notice the tell-tale signs of a lead vein and applied to Greenwich Hospital for a lease to work it on the same day. The resulting mine eventually proved very profitable for him. When he finally relinquished the lease, it was taken on by another company who had also initially applied to work the vein only a few hours after Walton. In this case, however, the 'early bird' had indeed caught the 'worm': the second company found very little and made a significant loss on their investment!

To the south-west of Garrigill, the sprawling fells culminate in the lofty plateau of Cross Fell. The lead-mining activity even extended onto these high and remote flanks, and the old 'corpse road' from Garrigill was upgraded to facilitate these developments. One of the key veins here was said to have been revealed by a horse pawing at the ground and so cutting through the turf. At an elevation of 700-750m, and particularly exposed to the wind, rain and snow of the high Pennines, conditions at these mines (Cashwell, Crossfell and Slate Sike) must have been very difficult for much of the year. The last mine in the district to close in 1948 was that at Rotherhope which is situated lower down in the valley of the Black Burn near to the small hamlet of Leadgate.

Although a tiny settlement now, Leadgate once had a large enough population to justify its own school, chapel and corn mill, as did Garrigill and the cluster of old buildings around Tynehead. Leadgate also marks the start of the route climbing out of South Tynedale towards the Eden valley (although the A686 follows a more direct route), ascending above Rotherhope Mine and the valley of the Black Burn to reach its summit at Hartside Cross. The remote valley of the Black Burn contains another of South Tynedale's impressive waterfalls at Cash Force, where the Whin Sill cuts across the stream bed to produce an interesting gorge with stepped cascades.

The River Nent is the major eastern tributary meeting the South Tyne at Alston: its Celtic name related to the Welsh word 'nant' used for a valley or river. The lower section of the river passes Gossipgate to reach Alston, flowing through attractive meadows with the waterfalls of Skelgill Force, the Seven Sisters and Nent Force. Much of the valley was once like this, tranquil and pastoral, until transformed by intense mining activity. Now, the mining has gone and the valley has been returned to its previous pastoral seclusion, no longer quite in its pristine state but contorted by the bumps, hollows and gashes of the old workings.

The village of *Nenthead* is situated at the top of the Nent valley where the road crossing from Weardale descends from its summit at Killhope Cross. An elevation of 440-460m above sea-level makes it one of the highest settlements in the country. Its rapid growth from a few dwellings into a large village is entirely attributable to the decision of the London Lead Company to establish their base and headquarters at this location.

Nenthead

In 1825 Nenthead became a 'planned village' for the mine-workers and by the time of the 1861 census, it had grown to 2000 inhabitants. The company influence meant the village featured some notable 'firsts', including the earliest place in the country to introduce compulsory education for children, and in 1833 the establishment of the first free library (the Reading Room still exists today). The company also built the large school (now the village hall) and provided for public bathing by building a wash-house. At Hillersdon Terrace, the distinctive houses were built for management officials and skilled technicians operating the smelt mill.

The presence of early mine workings around Nenthead is represented by the prominent gouges of Dowgang Hush and Greengill Hush to the south-west of the village, although earlier shafts on the fell date from the 17th century or before. These early excavations worked the obvious *lead veins*, but two key factors boosted further developments. Firstly, it was discovered in the later part of the 18th century that some of the *cross veins* that intersect the lead veins could also be very productive in the valley. Secondly, extensive 'flats' were found with large accessible mineral deposits that had spread out from the vein into the adjacent rock. Sometimes veins were considered worked out, such as in Old Carr's mine, then the miners would fortuitously break through into a zone of rich 'flats'. Often these 'flats' would be associated with a cavity, due to the greater density of the ore deposits compared to the original limestone, leaving behind a space as the mineral fluids consolidated.

Nentforce Level

Close by the River Nent at Alston is the obscured entrance to the famous Nentforce Level, sometimes also referred to as the 'Grand Aqueduct', and undoubtedly one of the major engineering feats of its time. Its development can be attributed to the mines in the Nent valley gradually probing deeper underground but being hindered by a lack of natural drainage. A proposal was therefore made to Greenwich Hospital by John Smeaton and Richard Walton to construct a subterranean level from Nent Force up the valley to Nenthead, with the twin objectives of 'unwatering the sills and discovering all veins which intersect the course of the said level'. Smeaton was a renowned engineer who also built the Eddystone lighthouse.

Work began on the level in 1776, but the original design was then modified to permit the use of barges after the intervention of the canal engineer John Gilbert. The barges facilitated the removal of waste which was then transferred at the level mouth onto tubs running on cast iron rails, probably used here for the first time instead of wooden rails. By 1818, the level had reached a shaft at Nentsberry Haggs, when economic imperatives meant the deep exploration was abandoned and the level continued after an intermediate vertical rise of 60m.

Sixty-six years later, and at a total cost of £81,000, the level reached Wellgill, near Nenthead (it was also later driven a further 1km to Rampgill Shaft). During the many years of construction it had become known as 'Smeaton's Folly' because only one significant ore vein was found. However, the investment was not completely wasted as the level succeeded in draining deep mine workings throughout the valley. Meanwhile, the canal passage had become a favourite boat excursion with both local people and visitors.

Nenthead Mines with the Assay House prominent on the left

In the vicinity of Nenthead, particularly rich veins occurred at Rampgill, Smallcleugh and Middlecleugh, with Longcleugh and Capelcleugh also very productive. Rather ironically, the Greenwich Hospital commissioners had decided not to lease out the Rampgill Vein but to work it themselves, expecting the same excellent results as found in nearby West Allendale. However, initial efforts were unproductive and the commissioners lost patience, eventually leasing the site to the London Lead Company, who drove a new horse level to facilitate a detailed exploration. They found an exceptionally rich vein, in places forming a rib up to 6m wide of solid ore.

Smallcleugh Mine was also very profitable with the discovery of an unusually good cross vein and extensive 'flats'. A cavern at Smallcleugh was later used for a celebrated dinner-dance by members of the local Masonic branch in 1901. Over time, the workings from the various mines became interconnected and, as the veins were followed north-east, some of the workings became contiguous with those from Coalcleugh in West Allendale.

Nenthead smelt mill dates from 1737, eventually becoming one of the most advanced operations in the region. By 1884 the site contained six ore-hearths, one slag hearth, two reverberatory furnaces, two refining furnaces and a desilvering house. The Assay House contained a laboratory where technicians would use their skill to determine whether the silver content of the ore would justify the additional refining required. A flue was built eastwards up the fell to a distant chimney (now collapsed) for removing fumes from the site. Water power for the mines and mill was provided by linked reservoirs at Perry's Dam and Smallcleugh, with a water leat for Perry's Dam extending 2km south across the fellside to intercept a much larger catchment.

Nenthead smelt mill closed in 1896 when the London Lead Company left the area. However, under the ownership of the Vieille Montagne Zinc Company, the dressing floors were further developed so that they could process about 200 tonnes of ore in 12 hours. In addition, the Brewery Shaft, which had been originally sunk to drain the horse level in Rampgill Mine through the Nentforce Level, was linked with new surface infrastructure thereby enhancing the head of water. Originally this new technology utilised steam-driven compressors but the reinstatement of water power then allowed the use of compressed air rock-drills. During the Vieille Montagne tenure, zinc became the primary ore, often by mining the 'dead' material used to 'pack out' the ends of worked-out veins.

Some of the surviving buildings associated with the Nenthead mines have been restored by the North Pennines Heritage Trust, providing an excellent opportunity to reconstruct the various processes and practices employed by the mining industry.

The entrance to the Mine Centre is on the site of the old Rampgill Mine and a little further up the stream beyond the reconstructed waterwheels is the remains of Nenthead Mill, with the Assay House marked by its prominent large chimney. A section of mine at Carr's Level has also been re-opened to the public in order to demonstrate the underground workings.

Smallcleugh (Handsome Mea) reservoir, Nenthead

Further down the Nent valley, Nentsberry had once been the principal settlement in the valley before Nenthead village was built. Rich veins were also found here at Gudham Gill, Brownley Hill and Nentsberry Haggs, with the workings extending up onto the shaft-peppered slopes of Whimsey Hill and over into the adjacent valley of Wellhope (West Allendale). To resolve the boundaries between the different landowners required accurate surveys, which were then demarcated on the ground by 'meerstones', many of them still existing today. At a later stage in the 20th century, an aerial ropeway linked the primary shaft at Wellhope with Nenthead Mill. The mine at Brownley Hill is widely-known because of the rare mineral discovered there, now called *alstonite*. As the Wellhope workings also link with Scraithole Mine at Carrshield, there is a story that the coffin of a deceased person was once brought underground from Carrshield to Nenthead for burial, together with mourners!

Skelgill Force on the River Nent below Blagill

South Tynedale Railway

The South Tynedale Railway

In the 19th century, the productivity and prosperity of the lead mines meant that Alston Moor was considered an attractive location to link into the developing railway network. At one stage the Stockton & Darlington Railway Company surveyed a potential route through Weardale with a planned tunnel at Killhope. However, it was the Newcastle & Carlisle Railway Company that eventually proceeded to build the line, connecting Alston with their existing Carlisle-Newcastle railway at Haltwhistle in 1852.

The topography necessitated some impressive engineering, notably the viaduct at Lambley, but also eight other bridges over the South Tyne or its tributaries. During the 20th century, despite the closure of many other rural branch lines, freight traffic maintained the viability of the South Tynedale railway. However, the closure of Lambley Colliery proved to be a major setback, and the line finally closed in 1976.

Nevertheless, events are now turning full circle: sterling efforts by dedicated volunteers from the South Tynedale Railway Preservation Society have reinstated parts of the line. Currently steam and diesel trains leisurely operate the four kilometres between Alston and Kirkhaugh, with plans also made for extending operations to Slaggyford. Meanwhile, the whole length of the route has become a pleasant walking route, known as the 'South Tyne Trail'.

The contrary nature of mining, whether adverse or providential, is particularly well displayed by the fortunes of Hudgill Burn Mine, near Nent Hall. Several previous trials here had discovered poor veins at considerable expense. Undiscouraged, John Wilson, Jacob Wilson and Company took up the lease in 1812 and with a team of experienced miners continued exploration. In 1814, this partnership had their 'lucky strike'. A series of rich veins was discovered that happened to converge at this locality, often with much cerrusite ('white lead') as well as galena, and frequently in a loose state, meaning relative easy working requiring no blasting. They also found a large cavity in the hillside about 300m long.

As a result of their exceptional discovery, all of the partners in the Hudgill Burn Company, including the miners who had shares, became very rich in a short period of time. John Wilson used some of this money to build the fine building of Nent Hall. A 19th century newspaper later wrote: 'when Hudgill Burn was at her best, more beer ran down the Nent Hall sewer to the Nent, than is drank in the whole parish now!'

In the lower section of the Nent valley, Corbygates takes its name from the old road which passed this way before crossing the fell by Blakelaw Cross en route for

Corbridge. The hillsides above Blagill are gouged and pitted with old hushes and shafts where another series of productive lead veins were found. It is possible that the name of Blagill comes from its connection with medieval German miners, 'Blei' being German for lead. The dressing floors for these mines are marked by the ruins and large tracts of spoil on the valley floor by the river. Overlooking the scene is the hill of Mounthooly, crowned by a prominent mast on its summit, and due to its location at the corner of the Nent and South Tyne valleys providing a commanding prospect of both valleys.

To the north of Alston, the South Tyne valley generally broadens out into a fertile valley floor formed from the alluvial 'haugh' lands of the river. Typically, the river flows across the floodplain in a series of multiple *braided* channels that are interwoven across a wide bed of shingle, the stony bed only becoming totally immersed when the river is in flood. Much of the alluvial gravel is a legacy of mining in the catchment, which left behind large quantities of unvegetated spoil to be washed into the streams. Analysis of the vertical profiles of the stream deposits has shown distinctive layers that can be related to episodes of deforestation and mining extending back into prehistory, including the 20th century switch from lead to zinc mining. Distinctive outcrops of fretted limestone also occur in the bed of the South Tyne near Randalholme.

At the junction of Ayle Burn with the South Tyne, the pele house at Randalholme has the archetypal thick walls and corner staircases but was later remodelled in the Renaissance style by the Whitfield family in 1650. The small side-valley of the Ayle Burn opening to the east is utilised by the A696 road heading towards Allendale and Hexham. At the top of this valley, the buildings of Leipsic and Moscow have their origins in the enforced farming of marginal land during the food shortages of the Napoleonic Wars. Clarghyll Hall is a curious mix of architectural styles, with a decorous pele tower dating from the 17th century, but built after it was really needed for defensive purposes.

The vicinity of Ayle has clear evidence of mining and quarrying, but without the great riches found elsewhere. Coal is also present, with the small Ayle and Clarghyll Collieries exploiting a narrow (0.5m thick) but productive seam in the rocks. During the course of workings at the Ayle Burn lead mine, an impressive water-worn natural cavern was discovered in the limestone strata. Due to the shallow thickness of limestone beds in the North Pennines, caves are not particularly common, but another system of subterranean passages does occur on the opposite side of the South Tyne valley at Tutman's Hole by the Gilderdale Burn. Coal was also worked from shallow pits in the same Gilderdale valley, high on the remote slopes of Hartside Height. Despite the remote location and thinness of the seams, as elsewhere in the Pennines, any source of coal was fully exploited.

Ramparts of the Roman fort at Whitley Castle

A little further downvalley is the curious landmark of Kirkhaugh church, which has a remarkable Bavarian-style slender spire that seems so thin that it must sway in high winds! A Bronze Age mound near here was found to contain a gold earring, possibly originating in Spain, as well as the more usual stone and flint tools.

Most of the buildings at Kirkhaugh are actually on the opposite river bank overlooked by the low hill on which stand the tiered Roman earthworks of Whitley Castle. Although no stonework is exposed at the fort, seven ramparts and ditches are visible on the west side and five such features on the north and south aspects; inscriptions have been found indicating that this was the one-time garrison of the 2nd cohort of the Nervii from the lower Rhine valley. Downvalley, the grounds of Barhaugh Hall form a charming area of parkland that further enhances this beautiful part of the valley: the name Barhaugh seems to be derived from 'bere' which suggests that barley was once grown on the local haugh land.

The largest settlement in this part of the valley is the attractive village of *Slaggyford*, which gets its name from the older version 'Slagginford', probably meaning 'muddy ford' and referring to a nearby crossing on the Knar Burn. The grouping of houses around the spacious village green reflect its original status as a market centre for the valley, eventually to be eclipsed by Alston's mining wealth. The nearby valley of Knarsdale, with its dispersed scattering of buildings was formerly a royal forest, and the present-day Knarsdale Hall is located on the site of a tower-house where the keeper of the forest resided.

The side-valleys on this western flank of South Tynedale are a intriguing mix of different influences: the 'dale' of Knarsdale is succeeded northwards by the more characteristic North Pennine 'hope' of Thinhope, and then further north is Glen Due which suggests more of a Scottish influence. The Roman route of the Maiden Way undulates over these western flanks from Whitley Castle to the Wall country, and this track was later adopted by the cattle drovers as one of their primary routes southwards.

The scenery of the lower part of South Tynedale is epitomised at Eals Bridge, where the river flows through attractive woodlands with a backdrop of steep bracken-covered slopes to the east. Downstream, the beautiful scenery continues amongst the sylvan setting of Oakeyside Wood and Hag Wood, leading to an abrupt constriction of the valley at Lambley. The railway surveyors utilised this narrowing to take the line across the valley from Lambley to Coanwood, but this still required the negotiation of a deep gap floored by the river.

The resulting structure of *Lambley Viaduct* was completed in 1852, spanning the valley with a total of sixteen spectacular arches and taking the railway line over 30m above the river. Although the trains have now gone, this magnificent monument to the railway age has been restored under the auspices of the North Pennines Heritage Trust. As a result, the viaduct and its surroundings can be appreciated both from its lofty parapets and from a woodland path with footbridge below.

Both Lambley and Coanwood had important coal mines that utilised the railway to transport their produce, but only ruins and derelict ground remain from these enterprises now. Below Coanwood, the fine riverside scenery continues to Featherstone Castle, with the river flowing through broad sweeping curves interspersed by large islands of shingle ('eals') around which the channel diverges. In some cases, the islands have become established long enough for a growth of shrubs and even woodland to develop, despite the periodic floods that sweep the river channel.

Featherstone Castle originally dates from the 13th century and was at that time an elaborate medieval tower-house, the home of the Featherstonehaugh family. As times and needs changed, much of the original has been subsumed by elaborate Jacobean modifications and Gothic flourishes from the 19th century. The castle stands in spacious parkland, interrupted in places by the broken remains of a former encampment, including its rusting gates. This was the site of Prisoner-of-War Camp 18, which was used to hold thousands of German prisoners between 1945 and 1948, many of whom also worked on local farms.

Williamston, near Slaggyford

Featherstone Castle

Lambley Viaduct

Featherstone Bridge

Bellister Castle

On the west riverbank, Bishop's Linn marks a final leap in the course of Glencune Burn before it joins the parent river. The riverside woodlands soon lead to the elegant structure of Featherstone Bridge, which dates from 1778; the great flood of 1771 had earlier destroyed all bridges upstream of Corbridge. Part of the charm of the bridge comes from its asymmetric span, necessitated by the differing heights of each bank: the arch keystone is clearly off-centre against the road platform above.

On the east side of the river, the small settlements of Featherstone Rowfoot and Park Village are the remaining villages before the bustle of the main Tyne Gap is reached at Haltwhistle. The last major tributary is the Park Burn which rolls off the declining swathes of moorland in typical Pennine fashion, creamy cascades alternating with a series of hidden gorges where the burn has cut deeply into the landscape.

A final highlight of the valley just to the south of the historic town of Haltwhistle is provided by *Bellister Castle*. The impressive ruins of the original 13th century fortification stand next to the newer house built by the Blenkinsopps in 1669: the latter was rebuilt in 1826 and is now managed by the National Trust. Both buildings stand on a raised *motte* feature and sections of moat can also be traced. The castle is best known for its legend of the Grey Man, the ghost of a minstrel killed by the master's hounds.

The River South Tyne sweeps around the jutting spur of Wydon Nab (an outcrop of the Whin Sill overlain by thick glacial sediments) to reach *Haltwhistle*, which clusters on its northern bank. The town has a long history as an important marketplace dating back to a license granted by King John in 1207. Frequent raids by the Border Reivers mean it is said to have more defensive houses than any other English town. The partly-hidden church of the Holy Cross (which is without a tower) is celebrated as one of the best examples of early English architecture. With the coming of the railway in the 1840s, Haltwhistle was also able to develop as a centre for mining, quarrying, and paint-making but now tourism associated with Hadrian's Wall occupies a key role in the local economy. The old viaduct over the Tyne on the South Tynedale railway has recently been restored as the 'Alston Arches'.

Back at Lambley, the main road (A689) diverges westwards from the main South Tyne valley, aiming for Brampton. The land becomes rougher and the outlook more austere as the road passes through a series of small villages on the bleak northern flanks of Cold Fell, last of the high Pennines. These villages, Halton-Lea-Gate, Midgeholme, Tindale and Hallbankgate share a common industrial heritage in that they grew up along the branch railway established by Lord Carlisle between

Lambley and Brampton. The villages therefore housed the workers employed in the coal mines, quarries (limestone and whinstone) and metal processing works that became established in this area. George Stephenson's famous 'Rocket' locomotive saw out its final days on a section of this railway line, moving wagons along one of the quarry inclines. At Hallbankgate there is a rather poignant memorial to three local people who died at the Roachburn coal mine in 1908, with the looser rock strata of the coal seams being more prone to collapses and flooding than in lead mines.

The metal works at Tindale were developed by James Attwood in 1845 to manufacture zinc metal (spelter) together with brass, copper, silver and nickel. There was a plentiful supply of local coal and Tindale Tarn was dammed to provide water power. Unfortunately, the high sulphur content of the waste fumes proved to have a severe effect on the surrounding land: by the 1880s, this required compensation of £65 per annum, and by 1893, 95 hectares of land had been destroyed by pollution with a further 61 hectares also adversely affected. Renewal of the company's lease therefore became conditional on reducing pollution, and Lady Carlisle also requested that the overcrowded workers' houses be upgraded. When the company declined to accept these conditions, the site was abandoned. Subsequently, an ill-fated attempt was made to re-start the industry in 1928 but it soon failed.

The rather austere outlook of the landscape remains today, but the prospect is mellowed by the large sheet of water at Tindale Tarn, ensconced in a secluded bowl at the foot of Cold Fell. This is a popular stop-over site for migrating birds and the Royal Society for the Protection of Birds has acquired a large sector of adjacent land to provide them with a relatively safe passage. Cold Fell is the most northerly hill of the high Pennines, forming a bleak and exposed swathe of inhospitable upland that usually justifies its harsh chilly description. It has, nevertheless, also apparently been titled as Coal Fell on account of the coal seams appearing on its flanks, with one of the small settlements below bearing this name too.

In addition to Cold Fell acting as the watershed between west-flowing streams heading for the Irish Sea, and east-flowing streams aiming for the North Sea, it also marks a divide in cultural terms. Streams to the west are 'becks', whilst to the east they are 'burns': the boundary in the vicinity of Tindale being quite distinct as the Howgill Beck and Coalfell Beck become transformed into the Haining Burn. This upland transition area has therefore functioned in the past as a human frontier as well as a physical boundary, with successive waves of settlement each leaving distinct traces on its fringes.

Tindale Tarn

Cold Fell

The 'mad river' in Gelt Woods

Geltsdale

Geltsdale Forest is an extensive tract of mountain ...... Part of it abounds in birch and alderwoods, and gives rise to the river Gelt
History, Gazetteer and Directory of Cumberland, Mannix & Whellan 1847

At the northernmost end of the Pennines, Geltsdale epitomises in its short length the distinctive appeal of these inimitable uplands. The River Gelt begins where two large streams meet, the Old Water and New Water, each draining a large area of high soggy fell. Their united waters then rush through 12km of helter-skelter descent to finally join the River Irthing close to its final meeting with the Eden. The name Gelt is suggested to be derived with good reason from the Norse word 'geilt', meaning it is the 'mad' or 'frenzied' river. Within the domain of its brief journey are compressed an exciting variety of scenery, a hidden cornucopia of wooded glades, dashing streams and wild moors.

The market town of *Brampton* is the main settlement in the near vicinity. Although it features the characteristic red sandstone buildings of the Eden valley, it also has strong links with the Tyne valley and the nearby Border area. The Romans built a fort nearby, located on the Stanegate just to the west of the present town, from where Hadrian's Wall could be defended if necessary. Foundations of a fortified medieval *motte* can also be seen on the prominent hillock above the town.

The Young Pretender, Bonnie Prince Charlie, stopped at Brampton in 1745 on his march south into England. When his army had completed the siege of Carlisle, the proud burghers of that city were forced to bring the gate keys across to him at Brampton. After the prince had later retreated back to Scotland, the burghers exacted their revenge: six notable supporters of the Jacobite cause were hung nearby at the Capon Tree. The existence of the tree is commemorated at a roadside plaque to the south-west of Brampton: its name comes from the capons eaten by judges who habitually halted under the large oak to regale themselves on the way to the Carlisle assizes, often accepting a few bribes in advance of proceedings!

Amongst the fine array of town buildings in Brampton are the house used by Bonnie Prince Charlie and the prominent octagonal-shaped Moot Hall with its ornamental cupola. The fortress-like St. Martin's Church, built in 1878, is renowned as the only ecclesiastical building designed by the Pre-Raphaelite architect Philip Webb; the church also contains a remarkable set of stained glass windows designed by Sir Edward Burne-Jones and produced in the studio of William Morris.

Brampton

In the rural hinterland south of Brampton is the very popular country park at *Talkin Tarn*, where a well-worn path encircles the lake through the fringing trees and shrubs. The tarn has no streams as feeders, but instead is supplied by underwater springs on the lake bed. Its origin can be attributed to formation as a 'kettle hole' feature, with the hollow being left behind by a large block of buried ice during the melting phase of the last Ice Age. Local legend tells of a drowned village lying beneath the waters of the tarn, with the toll of church bells sometimes emanating from beneath the turbulent waters on stormy nights.

Talkin Tarn

Geltsdale and Talkin Fell

The 'Written Rock of Gelt'

In the Gelt Quarries near Low Gelt Bridge is an inscription of particular interest, carved by a Roman soldier and referred to by Tennyson in his poem *'The Idylls of the King'*. The inscription is hard to find without expert knowledge but begins VEXILLATIO LEGIONIS SECUNDÆ. In translation it apparently consists of a series of statements lauding the achievements of *'A vexillation of the second legion, styled the August, on account of its bravery, under Agricola the optio [lieutenant]'* with *'Aper and Maximus being consuls'*. It also describes the quarry as being *'the workshop of Mercatius'*, suggesting that was the name of the person who carved the words, with the year given as 207AD.

Another Roman inscription has also been discovered a little higher up in Gelt Woods, on the opposite side of the river, but unfortunately this has been so severely weathered that it is virtually indecipherable.

Talkin Fell: looking to the Borderlands

The most dramatic and frenzied reaches of the River Gelt are in its lower section. This wild rush of water takes place in the rich setting of Gelt Woods, creating an enchanting landscape of great beauty. The river has carved a deep sinuous passage through a range of low knolls providing a succession of falls, rapids and pools, all carved from the colourful sandstone bedrock. When combined with the bewitching variety of woodland, this produces an exhilarating experience that changes with the rhythms of the seasons. A series of excellent paths thread the woods, twisting and turning over the knolls, providing excellent walking whatever the weather.

The chain of prominent sandstone quarries in Gelt Woods, now weathered with age, date back to Roman times. Stone from here was used to construct the fort near Brampton and to affect repairs to Hadrian's Wall. At a particular location in one of the quarries near to Low Gelt Bridge is the 'Written Rock of Gelt' where one of the Roman soldiers carved a Latin inscription, but this is by no means obvious. Also concealed in the quarries is the rudimentary hideaway of Abraham's Cave, which became a favourite den for those who lived beyond the law in the 19th century. A little further upstream, the main path though the woods crosses the Hell Beck where it meets the Gelt; this was the setting for a savage local battle back in 1570, after which the waters were said to have been stained red. The path then eventually leads to the Hayton-Talkin road where it passes under the Middle Gelt Viaduct. The lofty arches of the viaduct carry the Newcastle-Carlisle railway line and the bridge represents one of the earliest skew viaducts to be built anywhere in the world.

The upper valley of Geltsdale is masked by a broad ridge through which the river has cut a deep ravine. As a consequence, it tends to be hidden from external view and deeply enclosed by the surrounding fells in its middle reaches. The two settlements of Castle Carrock and Talkin provide the key to its entry, the former village providing the only road access, a cul-de-sac leading to the isolated lodge of Geltsdale House. The name of *Castle Carrock* is apparently derived from 'Castle Crag', a reference to an ancient fortification once built upon this site, but the village is now a large settlement straggling along the Brampton road. Hidden amongst the trees behind the village is a sizable reservoir built in 1902 to supply water for Carlisle.

Once the barrier is breached and the upper valley of the Gelt entered, the scene becomes more open, with the river flowing through fine woodlands backed by bracken and heather-covered fells. On the slopes of Talkin Fell, the lush grassland of The Greens marks the distinctive appearance of a band of limestone cutting across the hillside. The riverside alder woods are particularly attractive, with birch and rowan opportunistically taking root on the rocky slopes above. Although the area of woodland has been reduced from its former extent, the remainder has retained its vitality and continues to attract interesting and diverse wildlife. The crucial factor in its survival was that Geltsdale was The King's Forest, an ancient hunting ground reserved for the nobility. Under the strict jurisdiction of 'forest law', crimes such as tree-felling or poaching could be punished by death. For a long time in the Middle Ages, the Priory of Hexham held control over Geltsdale but at the time of Dissolution, the royal prerogative granted it to the barony of Gilsland.

Birds are particularly well-represented in the woods including warblers, woodpeckers, treecreepers and flycatchers, whilst the trees also provide sanctuary for animals such as red squirrels and roe deer. The recent involvement of the Royal Society for the Protection of Birds in managing the area will also hopefully mean greater success for the reintroduced hen harrier, as well as other birds of prey that have been ruthlessly persecuted in the past.

A series of delightful riverside paths lead through the woodlands to the confluence of the Old Water and New Water, passing a succession of rapids and pools on the river that are set amidst beautiful surroundings. A prominent feature by the riverbank is the massive quartzite boulder of the Gelt Stone, perched on its narrow keel next to the main valley path.

Beyond Binney Bank, the woodlands become more scattered and the heather moors begin to take over. The presence on the eastern flanks of the valley of a well-constructed track indicates the route to a series of old coal workings. Heather is unusually prevalent on these slopes for such a western situation, its existence being encouraged by the slightly lower rainfall totals compared to the high Pennines above the East Fellside. Nevertheless, the large lusty streams of the Old Water and New Water indicate that the highest ground stretching from Cold Fell to Croglin Fell is underlain by a morass of juicy peat, retaining its moisture in all conditions except extreme drought.

These upper reaches are remote, lonely terrain: as with much of the North Pennines, the demise of the old shielings and mine workings has meant that they are now considerably less frequented than in the past.

Bibliography

Addleshaw GWO 1954 *Blanchland: a short history.*
Auden WH 1994 *Collected Poems.* Faber & Faber.
Backhouse J 1896 *Upper Teesdale: Past and Present.*
Bellamy D & Quayle D 1992 *England's Last Wilderness.* Boxtree.
Bellamy D & Mackie S 1981 *The Great Seasons.* Hodder & Stoughton.
Bonser KJ 1970 *The Drovers.* Macmillan
Bowes P & Egglestone WM 1996 *Picturesque Weardale Revisited.* Weardale Publishing.
Bowes P & Wall T 1996 *Rookhope's Landscape Legacies.* North Pennines Heritage Trust.
Bradshaw ME (ed) 2003 *The Natural History of Upper Teesdale.* Durham Wildlife Trust. 4th edition.
Brook D *et al* 1988 *Northern Caves Volume1: Wharfedale and the North-East.* Dalesman.
Bulman R 2004 *Introduction to the Geology of Alston Moor.* North Pennines Heritage Trust.
Bulmer TF 1901 *History and Directory of Cumberland.*
Camden W 1590 *Britannica.* (Facisimile edition David & Charles 1971).
Chambers B (ed) 1992 *Men, mines and minerals of the North Pennines.* Friends of Killhope.
Chancellor FB 1954 *Around Eden: An anthology of fact and legend from and around the Eden Valley.* Whitehead & Son.
Charlton EM 1998 *Methodism in the Allen Dales.* North Pennines Heritage Trust.
Clapham AR (ed) 1978 *Upper Teesdale: The Area and its Natural History.* Collins.
Clark PAG & Pattison KE 1978. *Weardale chapels.* Dept. of Archaeology, Durham University
Coggins D (ed) 1996 *People and patterns: The carpet weaving industry in 19th century Barnard Castle.* Friends of the Bowes Museum.
Davies N 1999 *The Isles.* Macmillan.
Dixon H 1974 *An Allendale Miscellany.* Frank Graham.
Dunham KC 1990 *Geology of the North Pennine Orefield Vol. 1 Tyne to Stainmore.* 2nd edition. British Geological Survey.
Egglestone WM 1887-91 *Monthly Chronicle of North Country Lore and Legend.*
Egglestone WM 1887 *The projected Weardale Railway.* (Weardale Museum)
Emett C 2005 *Discovering the Eden Valley.* Sutton Publishing.

Fawcett JW 1902 *Tales of Derwentdale.*
Forbes I *Lead and Life at Killhope.* Killhope Lead Mining Museum.
Forbes I Young B Crossley C & Hehir L 2003 *Lead Mining Landscapes of the North Pennines.* Durham County Council.
Forster W 1883 *A Treatise on a Section of the Strata from Newcastle-upon-Tyne to Cross Fell.* 3rd edition (republished Davis Books 1985).
Forsythe R & Blackett-Ord C 1998 *Lambley Viaduct: History, Decline and Restoration of a Great Monument.* North Pennines Heritage Trust.
Graham JJ 1939 *Weardale: past and present.*
Hammond N 1998 *The Story of the Gaunless Valley: A North Pennine History.*
Hauxwell H & Cockroft B 1989 *Seasons of my Life.* Random Century.
Hauxwell H & Cockroft B 1990 *Daughter of the Dales.* Random Century.
Heatherington D *John Wesley: his journeys through Weardale 1752-1790.*
Higham N 1986 *The Northern Counties to AD 1000.* Longman.
Hill D 1996 *Turner in the North.* New Haven.
Hood K 2001 *Co-operative Societies of the North Pennines.* North Pennines Heritage Trust.
Hunt CJ 1970 *The Lead Miners of the North Pennines in the eighteenth and nineteenth centuries.* Manchester University Press.
Hutchison W 1794 *A History of the County of Cumberland.*
Kearney T 2004 *The Dark Side of the Dale.* Dark Side Publications.
Kristensen H 1999 *Memories of Hexhamshire.* Wagtail Press.
Lowe C 1997 *Plants of Upper Teesdale.* 2nd edition.
Lunn A 2005 *Northumberland. New Naturalist Series.* Harper Collins.
Manley G 1952 *Climate and the British Scene.* Collins
Mannix & Whellan 1847 *History, Gazeteer and Directory of Cumberland.*
Marshall JD 1981 *Portrait of Cumbria.* Robert Hale.
McCord N & Thompson R 1998 *The Northern Counties from AD 1000.* Longman.
Milburn TA 1987 *Life and times in Weardale 1840-1910.* Weardale Museum.
Mitchell WR 1967 *A Year with The Curlew: Life on the Northern Pennines.* Castleberg.
Mitchell WR 1979 *Pennine Lead-Miner. Eric Richardson of Nenthead: Personal Recollections of Life in the North Pennine Orefield.* Dalesman.
Mitchell WR 1988 *The Changing Dales: A Half-Century of Progress.* Dalesman.
Mitchell WR 1991 *High Dale Country.* Souvenir Press.

Myers A & Forsythe R 1999 *WH Auden: Pennine Poet*. North Pennines Heritage Trust.
Nixon P & Dunlop D 1998 *Exploring Durham History*. Breedon Books.
Palmer WT 1951 *Wanderings in the Pennines*. Skeffington & Son.
Parson & White 1829 *History, Directory and Gazetteer of the Counties of Cumberland and Westmorland*.
Pocock D 1990 *A History of County Durham*. Phillimore
Raistrick A 1968 *The Pennine Dales*. Eyre & Spottiswoode.
Raistrick A 1977 *Two centuries of Industrial Welfare: The London (Quaker) Lead Company 1692-1905*. 2nd edition. Moorland Publishing.
Raistrick A 1978 *Green Roads in the mid-Pennines*. Moorland Publishing.
Raistrick A & Jennings B 1965 *A History of Lead Mining in the Pennines*. Longmans.
Raistrick A & Roberts A 1984 *Life and Work of the Northern Lead Miner*. Beamish Museum.
Ramsden DM 1947. *Teesdale*. Museum Press
Ramsden DM 1948 *From Stainmore to the Tees*. Dalesman.
Ratcliffe D 2002. *Lakeland: The Wildlife of Cumbria. New Naturalist Series*. Harper Collins
Ridley N 1977 *Portrait of Northumberland*. 5th edition. Robert Hale.
Rollinson W 1978 *A History of Cumberland and Westmorland*. Phillimore.
Robertson A 2002. *A History of Alston Moor*. 3rd edition. Hundy Publications.
Robertson D & Keronka P 1991 *Secrets and Legends of old Westmorland*. Hayloft.
Robinson J 1999 *The Death and Life of a Dales Community: Harwood-in-Teesdale*.
Ryder P 1996 *Bastle houses in the North Pennines*. N Pennines Heritage Trust.
Sopwith R 2000 *Thomas Sopwith: The Allenheads Years 1845-1871*. North Pennines Heritage Trust.
Sopwith T 1833 *An Account of the Mining District of Alston Moor, Weardale and Teesdale* (republished Davis Books 1984).
Thain LM 1988 *Through the ages: the story of Nenthead*. North Pennines Heritage Trust.
Todd T *Autobiography of Thomas Todd of Middleton in Teesdale*.
Turnbull L 1975 *The History of Lead Mining in the North east of England*. Harold Hill & Son.
Utley D 1998 *The Helm Wind*. Bookcase.
Vyner B 2001 *Stainmore: Archaeology of a North Pennine Pass*. English Heritage.

Wainwright A 1967 *Pennine Way Companion* (republished Frances Lincoln 2004).
Wainwright A 1974 *Westmorland Heritage* (republished Frances Lincoln 2005).
Wainwright A 1986 *A Pennine Journey* (republished Frances Lincoln 2004).
Wallace W 1890 *Alston Moor: Its Pastoral People; Its Mines and Miners* (republished Davis Books 1986).
Wallace W 1890 *North Country Lore and Legend*. Walter Scott.
Walton P 1992 *The Stainmore & Eden Valley Railways*. Oxford Publishing.
Watson G 1974 *The Border Reivers*. Sandhill Press.
Watson G 1976 *Northumbrian Villages*. Robert Hale.
Weaver J 1992 *Exploring England's Heritage: Cumbria to Northumberland*. HMSO.
White P 1967 *Portrait of County Durham*. Robert Hale.
Williams LA 1975 *Road transport in Cumbria in the 19th century*. Allen & Unwin.
Wilkinson A 1998 *Barnard Castle: Historic Market Town*. Smith Settle.
Wilkinson P 2002 *The Nent Force Level and Brewery Shaft*. North Pennines Heritage Trust.

British Mine Research Society Monographs:
Fairbairn RA 1993 *The Mines of Alston Moor*.
Fairbairn RA 1996 *Weardale Mines*.
Fairbairn RA 2000 *Allendale, Tynedale and Derwent Lead Mines*.
Pirt WK & Dodds JM 2002 *Lead mining in the Derwent Valley*.
Fairbairn RA 2005 *The Mines of Upper Teesdale*.

Buildings of England series (Yale University Press):
Pevsner N & Williamson E 2002 *County Durham*.
Pevsner N et al 2002 *Northumberland*.
Pevsner N 2002 *Cumberland & Westmorland*.
Pevsner N 2002 *Yorkshire: The North Riding*

Walking Guides:
Regular guides are produced by a range of publishers including Cicerone, Questa, Hillside and Dalesman, in addition to local pamphlets available from information centres and visitor centres. The following provide distinctive perspectives:
Lowe C & Lowe G 2005 *Wild Flower Walks of Upper Teesdale*. Dales Country.
Welsh M 2001 *Waterfall Walks: Teesdale and the High Pennines*. Cicerone Press.

Index

Allen Banks, 124
Allen Mill, 117
Allendale Town, 117
Allenheads, 113
Alston, 129
Alston Moor, 10, 16, 129
Appleby, 31
Argill, 24
Armathwaite, 11
Ashgill Force, 8, 131
Auden, WH, 5
Augill, 24
Ayle, 139
Baldersdale, 61
Barhaugh, 139
Barnard Castle, 49
Barras, 24
bastles, 16
Bearsbridge, 123
Belah valley, 24
Bellister Castle, 142
Beltingham, 124
Birkdale, 76
Blackett Level, 116
Blagill, 139
Blanchland, 102
Blencarn, 41
Bollihope, 7, 17, 85
Border Reivers, 15
Bowes, 50
Bowlees, 69
Brampton, 145
Brignall Banks, 52
Brough, 15, 27
Bullman Hills, 11

Burnhope Resv., 95
Carriers, 118
Carrshield, 121
Castle Carrock, 146
castles, 15
Catton, 118
Cauldron Snout, 76
caves, 12
Coalcleugh, 119
Coanwood, 140
Cold Fell, 142
Cotherstone, 11, 58
Cotman, John Sell, 49
Cow Green Resv., 76
Cowshill, 95
Croglin, 46
Cronkley, 74
Cross Fell, 2, 12, 38, 129, 134
Cross Fell Inlier, 7, 33
Cumrew, 46
Cupola, 123
Deepdale, 11, 58
Derwent Mines, 105
Derwent Resv., 99
Devil's Water, 107
Dickens, Charles, 50
Dipton Mill, 110
drove roads, 16, 107
Dufton, 33
Eastgate, 90
Edmundbyers, 99
Eggleston, 12, 15, 62
Egglestone Abbey, 57
Egglestone, WM, 83
enclosures, 16

Featherstone Castle, 140
Forster, Westgarth, 130
Frosterley, 85
Frosterley Marble, 9, 85
Gamblesby, 42
Garrigill, 131
Gaunless Mill, 63
Gelt Woods, 146
Gibson's Cave, 70
God's Bridge, 50
Great Dun Fell, 12, 38
Greta Bridge, 53
Hallbankgate, 142
Haltwhistle, 12, 142
Hamsterley Forest, 84
Harthope Quarry, 9
Hartley, 24
Hartside Cross, 42
Harwood, 72, 74
haughs, 13
Hauxwell, Hannah, 61
Heatheryburn cave, 14
Helbeck Fell, 27
Helm Wind, 40
Hexham, 109
Hexhamshire, 100
High Cup Nick, 10, 35
High Force, 71
Hilton, 33
Holwick, 70
Hudeshope, 67
Hunstanworth, 106
Ireshopeburn, 94

Jingle Holes, 27
Killhope, 96
Kirkby Stephen, 26
Kirkcarrion, 65
Kirkhaugh, 139
Kirkland, 41
Kirkoswald, 42
Knarsdale, 139
Knock Fell, 38
Lady Anne Clifford, 32
Lambley, 140
Langdon Beck, 72
Langley Castle, 127
Langley Mill, 126
Langleydale, 57
Lartington, 58
lead mining (gen.), 17
lead veins, 10
Leadgate, 134
Limestone Brae, 121
Long Meg, 14, 42
Low Force, 69
Lunedale, 11, 12, 63
lynchets, 15
Maiden Castle, 21
Maiden Way, 14
Martin, John, 126
Marwood Chase, 57
Meeting of the Waters, 54
Melmerby, 41
Mickle Fell, 75
Mickleton, 63
Middleton, 65
Midgeholme, 9, 142

Milburn, 37
Moking Hurth, 14, 72
monasteries, 16
Monk, 123
Moor House, 78
Mortham Tower, 54
Mounsey, William, 45
Muggleswick, 100
Murton, 11, 33
Nenthead, 135, 137
Newbiggin (Eden), 46
Newbiggin (Tees), 69
Nine Standards, 26
Ninebanks, 122
Ousby, 41
peles, 16
Pikelaw, 3, 70
Plankey Mill, 124
quarrying, 18
Queen's Cave, 110
Raby Castle, 58
religion, 19, 95, 121
Renwick, 42
Rey Cross, 21
Riddlehamhope, 106
Rokeby Park, 54
Romaldkirk, 58
Rookhope, 7, 90
Scordale, 33
Scott, Sir Walter, 53
Sinderhope, 116
Sipton, 115
Skirwith, 41
Slaggyford, 139
Sleightholme, 52
Slitt Wood, 93

Sneep, The, 100
Sopwith, Thomas, 115
South Tynedale Railway, 138
St. John's Chapel, 93
Staindrop, 57
Stainmore, 9, 12, 21
Stanhope, 87, 88
Stanhope & Tyne Railway, 88
Staward Pele, 124
Stenkrith, 26
Swindale, 24
Swinhope, 115
Talkin Tarn, 145
Tan Hill, 23
Teesdale flora, 68
Tindale, 142, 143
Tunstall Reservoir, 83
Turner, JMW, 49
Tynehead, 133
Wallace, William, 130
Warcop, 27
Watson, Richard, 66
Wearhead, 95
Wesley, John, 95
Westgate, 92
Whin Sill, 10
Whitfield, 123
Whitley Castle, 14
Whorlton, 57
Widdybank, 7, 75
Winch Bridge, 69
Winton, 24
Wolsingham, 81
Wyclif, John, 57

150

Useful Contacts

Intake Force, Belah valley

The North Pennines Heritage Trust
Nenthead Mines Heritage Centre, Nenthead, Alston, Cumbria CA9 3PD
http://www.npht.com
Works to conserve the historic remains of man's activities in the landscape and to help people enjoy and understand them.

Durham Wildlife Trust
Rainton Meadows, Chilton Moor, Houghton-le-Spring, Tyne & Wear DH4 6PU
http://www.durhamwildlifetrust.org.uk

Northumberland Wildlife Trust
St Nicholas Park, Gosforth, Newcastle upon Tyne, Tyne & Wear NE3 3XT
http://www.nwt.org.uk

Cumbria Wildlife Trust
Plumgarths, Crook Road, Kendal, Cumbria LA8 8LX
http://www.wildlifetrust.org.uk/cumbria

North Pennines AONB Partnership
Weardale Business Centre, 1 Martin St., Stanhope, Co. Durham DL13 2UY
http://www.northpennines.org.uk

East Cumbria Countryside Project
Warwick Mill, Warwick Bridge, Carlisle CA4 8RR
http://www.eccp.org.uk

Royal Society for the Protection of Birds (RSPB)
1 Sirius House, Amethyst Road, Newcastle Business Park, Newcastle NE4 7YL
http://www.rspb.org.uk

Forestry Commision (Hamsterley)
http://www.forestry.gov.uk/hamsterleyforest

Friends of Killhope
http://www.killhope.co.uk

John Muir Trust http://www.jmt.org